THE MYSTERY OF CHRIST IN YOU

THE
MYSTERY
OF CHRIST
IN YOU

◊

The Mystical Vision of Saint Paul

GEORGE A. MALONEY, SJ

ALBA·HOUSE house NEW·YORK

SOCIETY OF ST. PAUL, 2187 VICTORY BLVD., STATEN ISLAND, NEW YORK 10314

ST PAULS

Unless otherwise noted, all scripture quotations are taken from *The New Testament and Psalms* (New York: Alba House, 1998), translated by Mark Wauck and used with permission.

Library of Congress Cataloging-in-Publication Data

Maloney, George A., 1924-
    The mystery of Christ in you: the mystical vision of Saint Paul /
George A. Maloney.
        p.   cm.
    Includes bibliographical references.
    ISBN 0-8189-0802-5
    1. Paul, the Apostle, Saint. 2. Mystical union — Biblical
teaching. 3. Jesus Christ — History of doctrines — Early church, ca.
30-600. 4. Bible. N.T. Epistles of Paul — Theology.   I. Title.
BS2655.M85M35   1998
225.9'2 — dc21   97-27145
                                                      CIP

Imprimi Potest
Rev. Edward Mathie, SJ
Provincial of the Society of Jesus
Wisconsin Province
1996

Produced and designed in the United States of America by the
Fathers and Brothers of the Society of St. Paul,
2187 Victory Boulevard, Staten Island, New York 10314,
as part of their communications apostolate.

ISBN: 0-8189-0802-5

Printing Information:

Current Printing - first digit   1   2   3   4   5   6   7   8   9   10

Year of Current Printing - first year shown

1998   1999   2000   2001   2002   2003   2004   2005   2006   2007

DEDICATION

To Doctor Chris Matthews

A Modern Disciple of St. Paul
Who Preaches Christ Crucified
As a Medical Doctor

ACKNOWLEDGMENTS

Sincere thanks to Cyndy Murphy, Ray Miles,
Sister Rita Trudell, CSJ, assistant librarian of
St. Joseph Center Library, Orange, CA
and June Culver for her generous assistance.

TABLE OF CONTENTS

INTRODUCTION

— ◊ —

In the Basilica of St. Paul Outside the Wall in Rome there is an inscription above the "altar of the confession" that expresses the whole message of St. Paul in his own words: "For to me life is Christ, and death is gain" (Ph 1:21). Paul more than any other early sacred writer beheld Christ immersed in and energizing the created, material world. Christ is shown as the center of unity for all that has been created. Paul would wish to lead us high up on the mountain of faith to gaze over the whole universe below.

If we have his faith, we shall see Christ as the center and focal point toward whom and from whom all created beings flow. Christ is not to be separated from material reality. All reality is already christologically structured by the incarnation whereby God inserted himself into his creation.

In Christ

Paul had received from the Lord himself the central doctrine of Christianity concerning our human incorporation into Christ's own life, hence into our very being. As the Apostle to the Gentiles, he boldly developed this key teaching that made Christianity essentially different from paganism. Through the cross Christ destroyed eschatological death and sin. By his own resurrectional life he has brought to us this "new life" (Rm 6:10-11). For us to become alive to God in Christ Jesus, we must be united with Christ. We must live "in Christ."

St. Paul is one of the most original, most personal, most powerful human personalities in the New Testament writings. You may not understand him, at least in some of his teachings. You may not even like him through his teachings. On the other hand, you might be humbled before the Apostle, the persecutor of early Christians, converted suddenly as he was "seized" by Jesus (Ph 3:12) in vision on the road to Damascus (Ac 9:1-9; 22:17-21). You might regard him as the most zealous Christian missionary who ever lived, someone who could boast in the Lord that he expended himself more than anyone else in his great zeal to preach Jesus Christ crucified:

> Are they servants of Christ? Now I'm speaking like a madman — I am even more so! I've worked harder, spent more time in prison, been beaten more severely, and have often been in danger of death. Five times I received forty lashes less one from the Jews, three times I was beaten with rods, once I was stoned, three times I was shipwrecked — a day and a night I spent out on the deep! In my many journeys I've been in danger from rivers, from robbers, from my own race, from Gentiles; I've been in danger in the city and in the wild, on the sea and from false brothers. I've toiled and been through hardships, spent many sleepless nights, been hungry and thirsty; I've often gone without food, been cold and without sufficient clothing. And apart from these external things, I experience daily cares and anxiety for all the churches (2 Cor 11:23-27).

I hope whoever reads this, would wish not to ignore St. Paul, who developed so much of the teachings, theology and piety that make up true Christianity. Every author who has attempted to write a book about St. Paul must have an "angle" or a special approach, since Paul is so deep in insights, so challenging to all Christians of all ages, so deeply in love with Christ and the members of his Body, the Church.

Paul's Mystical Vision

My "angle" — one which has always intrigued me about Paul's writing — is his fiery yet intimate, passionate yet humble and practical love for Jesus Christ. This underlies Paul's constant preaching and writing to his recent converts concerning the union of each and every Christian with Christ Jesus. Thus my approach is to try to make Paul's "mystical vision" of our mysterious indwelling union with Jesus Christ — true God and true Man, risen in glory yet united as Head to the living members of his Body, the Church — as easy to understand as possible.

Paul's personal union with Christ grew continually in intensity as he powerfully preached this good news. He suffered more than we can imagine in his efforts to bring his "gospel," the good news of God's *mysterion* — the incomprehensible mystery of God's eternal plan of salvation for all human beings in Jesus Christ through the working of the Holy Spirit — to Jewish and Gentile converts alike.

Paul's Understanding of Mysticism

Paul would never have considered himself a "mystic" or a preacher of "mysticism" according to the limitations we tend to put on these terms to describe any kind of union with the ineffable Triune God. Modern authors who write on the subject of mysticism usually highlight the subjective, ecstatic and deeply emotional experiences (often considered extraordinary) that are given to special persons but not available to all. Paul continually experienced the reality of the mystery he lived as something natural to Christians. He talked of it as a permanent union in and with Christ that would never cease growing.

Chapter One lays the foundation of Paul's understanding of our mystical union with Christ. This is what he calls the *mystery* or *mysterion* (in Greek). It is the pivotal revealed truth around which Paul preached and wrote concerning the key elements of Christ's teaching on such things as salvation, redemption, sanctification, faith, hope and love, divine filiation, the Body of Christ, the Church, ethical values, prayer, suffering, the apostolate, etc.

Chapter Two develops Paul's understanding of the phrase he used 164 times, "to live *in Christ.*" This reality of the individual Christian and all the members of the Church is central to the development of Paul's theology of redemption and our own incorporation in Christ through the Spirit of Jesus risen. We become children of God by our life in Christ. Baptism immerses us into this union with the resurrected and glorious Christ. We are reconciled to God in Christ Jesus through Baptism (Rm 5:11). From that point on, Christ journeys in us and with us through the power of the Holy Spirit, who gives us new gifts, all for the same purpose, to build up the Body of Christ which is the Church (1 Cor 12:4-11).

Chapter Three offers a deeper look into the meaning of our union *in Christ* and the many ramifications of this mystery in our earthly existence. We see it as a reality that comes about through Christ's death and resurrection. Christ calls us and empowers us to choose to live in this dynamic of death-resurrection by the working of the Holy Spirit. It is a summary of Paul's teachings on the Christian life. In it we see Paul's practical sense in stressing the fruit of our real union in Christ which must always be measured by our efforts *in the Holy Spirit* to die to the "old creation" and live in the "new creation" by our own efforts to build up the Body of Christ.

This leads us in Chapter Four to trace Paul's teaching on how concretely Christians come into this union with Christ and, in him, to union with the Father and the Holy Spirit. We see the importance of Baptism and the other sacraments which initiate us into this "new life" and aid us through self-discipline to grow daily in the tension of the *already* and the *not yet*. This is where Paul teaches us about spiritual combat or what later in Christianity came to be known as asceticism.

Chapter Five develops Paul's theology of the Holy Spirit and his work in empowering us to live in the indwelling Trinity as we seek to use the Spirit's special gifts or *charismata* apostolically to build up the Body of Christ.

This prepares us to examine in Chapter Six Paul's teachings on the Mystical Body of Christ, the Church. Paul brings us to see that our new life in Christ moves in a dynamic progressive way, both on the individual and the communal level of one's apostolate to help build up the Christian community.

Paul saw both areas as two views of the same reality, union in Christ. I present in Chapter Seven a gathering of texts that highlight Paul's personal experiences of the *mystery*. In the course of his life, he received extraordinary insights into this mystery that helped him in his own spiritual growth and enlightened him in his apostolic labors to know the divine secret revealed in this or that moment that touched on the plan of salvation of the world through Christ. Paul received mystical experiences of great supernatural import, but he used them not for his own personal gain but as God's gifts in his apostolate to win all human beings to Christ. We are challenged by Paul to rethink what true mysticism should mean for all Christians.

The End Times

Christianity has always preached, as Paul did, an eschatological theology concerning the finality of God's plan of salvation and the end of this material world. In Chapter Eight we see how Paul's writings show two specific, eschatological emphases.

The first he developed in his earliest writings, the 1st and

2nd Epistles to the Thessalonians (written about the end of 51 or the beginning of 52 AD). Paul's early emphasis on an imminent Second Coming of Christ, whom the Thessalonians were expecting to return at any moment to take them to be with him in heaven, was an exhortation to live with joyful expectancy for Christ's coming, but not to be overly concerned with the exact time.

The second and more important emphasis highlights the cosmic dimensions of Christ's redemption, namely to "reestablish" all creatures in their lost unity and bring them all back to the Father. This emphasis is developed in his last epistles to the Colossians (c. 61-63, written in Rome during his last captivity) and to the Ephesians (c. 61-63).

Paul here develops his teachings on the *pleroma* or the fullness of Christ in his resurrectional personhood, bringing to perfection the divine life which Christ bestows upon his living members in his Body. At the *parousia* the fulfillment of God's plan of salvation will be manifested. *Parousia* for Paul refers to the final "appearance" of Christ's ultimate triumph in and through his Body, the Church. Members of Christ's Body, filled with the hopeful expectancy of Christ's final coming, have, according to Paul, a great responsibility to work in and through the risen Savior to bring about the Lord's final coming in glory.

One of Paul's greatest contributions to Jewish eschatology is the concept that the destiny of the entire cosmos is one with our human destiny as we and the cosmos will be brought to completion by Christ, the Redeemer (1 Cor 15:24-28) when he hands all things over to the heavenly Father. Only then will Christ's triumphant victory over sin and death be completed. Only after Christ has presented the Kingdom to the heavenly Father will God be "all in all" (1 Cor 15:28).

Our Lives Are Hidden in Mystery

Each of us lives a life that is hidden in mystery. We look back to past experiences and can identify many instances in which the love of very special persons were instrumental in our growth as unique persons. Such experiences could never be willed; they form part of the *mystery of love.* There were likewise times when we experienced the *mystery of rejection* by others and the darkness of our own brokenness and sin. Our relationship with the Trinity, the Burning Bush never consumed, unfolds in the mystery of ever deeper faith, hope and love.

Our life in Christ is a true *mystery,* made up by the infusion of the Holy Spirit during times of light and illumination. Then there follows in our living of the *mystery* the shadows where his indwelling in us seems undefinable, neither present nor absent. The circle is completed by darkness wherein Christ seems to be totally absent. To run away from the *mystery of Christ in us* is to leave the desert and return to the "fleshpots" of slavery.

In the Book of Wisdom we read these words: "In the time of their visitation they will shine forth and will run like sparks through the stubble" (Ws 3:7; NRS). These words could easily describe the story of Paul who lived in Christ amidst so many trials, persecutions, and battles with himself and others until at last he could say that it was no longer he who lived but Christ who lived within him (Gal 2:19-20). May this book help you to live the *mystery of Christ in you* that you, like Paul, may "shine forth" the mystery of your life in him and "run like sparks through the stubble."

Pentecost: 1997
George A. Maloney, SJ

THE MYSTERY OF CHRIST IN YOU

1

LIVING IN THE MYSTERY

◊

KARL RAHNER has insisted that only those who experience God will continue to grow as human beings and hence as truly religious persons. "The devout Christian of the future will either be a 'mystic,' one who has 'experienced' something or he will cease to be anything at all."[1] Mysticism is a phenomenon that is rapidly sweeping the world during the second half of this twentieth century. It takes many forms which should convince us of a basic hunger in all of us human beings for an intimate relationship with the Divine.

In all of us there exists a propensity toward union with God. If we call that Supreme Reality God, we are saying that all other finite beings must ultimately fail to satisfy our thirst for deeper, more intense interpenetration with God. Intrinsic to an authentic mysticism is the accent on the conscious awareness of a subject brought progressively into a more intense, assimilating union with the ineffable, transcendent God. In such a mystical union we move away from any Cartesian duality of subject and object in order to experience God as the very inner force within us and all around us, supporting all being in God's mighty but gentle, transcendent but immanent, creative love.

---

[1] Karl Rahner, *Theological Investigations*, Vol. VII (NY: Seabury, 1971), p. 15.

1

None of us human beings can know this awesome *Plenitude of Being* through the shadow realities of intellectual concepts. For the living God cannot be forced into our human, objective categories. It is in dying to human "knowledge about" God that we begin to experience God with a "knowledge of" the invisible, but real presence of God. The Isha and Kena Upanishads of the Hindus exhort us to transcend all objective human knowledge, as well as sheer ignorance, in order truly to know God:

> He is not known by him who knows him,
> Not understood by him who understands.
> He alone contemplates him who has ceased to
>   contemplate him....
> It is in knowing him alone that one becomes immortal.
> A great loss it is, in truth, for him who does not attain him
> here below.[2]

Meaning of the Word, "Mysticism"

We must first recognize that there is no single, universally accepted definition of *mysticism.* David Knowles, O.S.B., warns us: "Everyone in our day who proposes to speak or write of mysticism must begin by deploring both the ambiguity of the word itself and the difficulty of defining it in any of its meanings."[3]

Christian mysticism finds its roots in the Jewish biblical experience in which "a direct encounter with God often characterizes the lives of the patriarchs, the prophets and women of faith."[4] It is in and through the mysticism that Jesus experi-

---

[2] *The Isha Upanishad,* cited by Swami Abhishiktanada, in *Hindu-Christian Meeting Point Within the Cave of the Heart* (Bombay: Bandra, 1969), p. 56.

[3] David Knowles, OSB, *What Is Mysticism* (London, 1967).

[4] John Welch, O.Carm., "Mysticism," in Joseph A. Komonchak et al, *The New Dictionary of Theology* (Washington, DC: Catholic University Press, 1968), p. 695.

enced in his earthly life as recorded in the New Testament that we can come somewhat to understand the full scope of Christian mysticism and even to experience the unity and diversity of sharing the Trinitarian divine life of grace as we live in Christ and he lives in us.

Therefore Jesus Christ, who through his Spirit divinizes us by making us "participants in God's very own nature" (2 P 1:4), is our model.[5] We Christians share in his own life, that life of the historical person, Jesus Christ, now gloriously resurrected. We become personally incorporated into Christ without losing our own identity. Christ lives in us, yet the intensity of union between ourselves and him is always an ongoing process of growth as "from glory to glory" we become formed in his image and likeness. "Those God knew beforehand he also predestined to be conformed to the image of his Son, so that he might become the firstborn of many brothers" (Rm 8:29).

Paul's Mystical Realism

Paul never used our term, *mysticism*. Especially he never understood the various meanings we modern Christians attach to it. When we use the word *mystical* we usually imply some extraordinary, charismatic gifts and special religious experiences, filled with much feeling. The experiences imply a large measure of subjectivity and by their nature are exceptional. Yet Paul did not consider the doctrine of the incorporation and transfiguration of the Christian into Christ through his divinizing grace and our cooperation as something esoteric, a delicacy reserved for only a few.

For Paul, every Christian turning away from his or her sinful past in a true *metanoia*, a conversion and total surrender of one's whole being in which the indwelling Trinity becomes the

---

[5] *Ibid.*

very Center of one's existence, enters into a permanent union of life in and with Christ. We become mature Christians only as long as we consciously live in this union with Christ through the power of the Spirit and his gifts of faith and love. Such a reality is attained by faith, as the Savior himself said before his ascension into glory: "He who believes and is baptized will be saved" (Mk 16:16).

The mere example of Christ derived from the Gospels and his ideas do not operate on us in some vague, impersonal way. The very historical person of Jesus Christ indwells the baptized Christian as a spiritual, yet personal power. This is the mysterious dynamic behind what it means to be baptized in Christ and possessed by his person. Paul used the terms "apprehended" or "seized" by Christ (Ph 3:12), to indicate that the principle of his thoughts, words and deeds was no longer Paul, the "natural" man, subjected to the laws of the flesh and sin, but Christ "who lives in me" (Gal 2:20). It is the Christ who died on the cross and rose from the dead, the Christ of history, who lives in him.

Paul seized on the reality of this relationship to Christ and never tired of seeking different metaphors to convey its vivid truth. He speaks of the life of Christ within the Christian as a new life that must be put on, not by a few, but by all Christians.

> For all of you who were baptized into Christ have clothed yourselves with Christ. There is neither Jew nor Greek, there is neither slave nor free, there is neither male nor female — you are all one in Christ Jesus (Gal 3:27-28).

To "put on Christ" is to become surrounded by him. This relationship to Christ is not merely moral; it is ontological, a "mystery" accepted in the faith and love of the Holy Spirit, a real union in love that differentiates as it unites.

Paul's Use of the Word, "Mysterion"

Paul uses the Greek word *mysterion* twenty-one times.[6] Scholars have long disputed whether Paul was influenced by the language and doctrine of the mystery cults of Asia Minor and the Hellenistic cults derived from the gods of Samothrace (Cybele, Attis, Adonis) and the Egyptian deities Isis and Osiris.[7] There can be no doubt that Paul knew the popular mystery cults of his day where the word *mysterion* or mystery referred to a secret ceremony or a truth to be kept concealed by those initiated into the "mysteries" that gave them a privileged *gnosis* or enlightenment.[8] But in all the cases where Paul uses the word, *mysterion*, he gives it his own Christian meaning.

Paul uses this term to refer to the hidden work of God's decrees to save humankind as applied specifically to Christ, who completes salvation in himself. Wikenhauser describes the mystical union with Christ and in Christ in the mystery of God's salvific plan in these words: "For Paul also, fellowship with Christ is marked by the fact that man is in Christ and Christ is in man. Paul uses both expressions: 'in Christ' and 'Christ in us.' But 'in Christ' is much the more common of the two."[9] We will expand on this in the next chapter. Paul in his First Epistle to the Corinthians writes to convince them of a new kind of Christian wisdom as opposed to the *Gnostic* wisdom that the Hellenic Jews had brought into their interpretation of mainline Judaism from the mystery cults of Asia Minor. He says, "When I came to you, I didn't proclaim the mystery of God to you in high-sounding language or with a display of wisdom. I had made

---

[6] Alfred Wikenhauser, *Pauline Mysticism. Christ in the Mystical Teaching of St. Paul* (NY: Herder & Herder, 1956), p. 18.

[7] For a detailed study of the mystery cults, cf. Gerhard Kittel, ed., *Theological Dictionary of the New Testament* (Grand Rapids, MI: Wm. B. Eerdmans Co., 1995), Vol. IV, art., *Mysterion*, by G. Bornkamm, p. 802 ff.

[8] On the subject of gnosis in relation to the mystery religions, cf. Kittel, ed., *op. cit.*, Vol. I, art., *Gnosis*, by R. Bultmann, pp. 689-714.

[9] Wikenhauser, p. 19.

up my mind to know nothing while I was among you except
Jesus Christ, and the fact that he was crucified" (1 Cor 2:1-2).
Christ, as Paul insisted, had taught them a way of living based
on true *agape*, or love. This is true wisdom that comes, not
from our own human striving, but as a sheer gift given by the
Holy Spirit:

> Yet among the mature we do preach wisdom, but a wis-
> dom which is not of this age nor of the rulers of this
> age.... Instead we preach God's wisdom, a wisdom which
> is *mysterious*, hidden, which God ordained before the
> ages for our glory (1 Cor 2:6-7).

Such true wisdom can come only from God because it
must be God's revelation that brings us into knowledge of the
mystery of his saving decrees from all eternity. This wisdom
comes to the humble and poor in spirit who are open to receive it from the Holy Spirit. It is the Holy Spirit who plunges
into the depths of everything, even into the depths of God himself (cf. 1 Cor 2:12). Thus Paul tells the Corinthians and ourselves today: "And we proclaim this in words taught by the Spirit
rather than by human wisdom, words which explain spiritual
realities to those who have the Spirit" (2:13).

God's revelation is mediated to us by human teachers, especially the first Apostles, including St. Paul (1 Cor 1:17). Thus
we Christians are new beings, now living in Christ and his Spirit
(1:30). This is a sheer gift coming out of God's initiative since
the knowledge, the true revelation and the language used to
lead us into God's mystery in Christ have to come from God.
We see this clearly in one of the letters Paul wrote while he
was in captivity, the epistle to the Ephesians, where he gives
one of the clearest expressions of what he means by the concept of the *mysterion*:

> Blessed be the God and Father of our Lord Jesus Christ,
> who has blessed us in Christ with every spiritual bless-

ing in the heavens. He chose us in Christ before the foundation of the world to be holy and blameless before him. In his love, he destined us beforehand to be his adopted sons through Jesus Christ, according to the purpose and desire of his will, to the praise of the glorious grace that he bestowed upon us in his beloved (Eph 1:3-6).

The mystery of God's salvific plan begins with the gratuitous choice God has made of us. "Through Christ's blood we are redeemed and our sins are forgiven — such is the wealth of his grace which he has poured out upon us" (Eph 1:7-8). "He has made known to us the *mystery* of his will, according to the purpose that he set forth in him" (1:9). What humility we must show to God as we respond to live "in Christ" by putting off the old man and being renewed in mind and spirit (4:22-23)! Such divine predilection implies a certain exclusiveness. Yet what has been revealed to us in the mystery of Christ is meant by God to include, not only the conversion of the Jews and the Gentiles of the world in which Paul lived, but also every human being of all times and places, male and female, all made in the image and likeness of God (Gn 1:26-27).

We all have a destiny: to be holy and blameless before God (Eph 1:4). We have been individually chosen to enter into the Kingdom of God by even now sharing in God's very own nature (2 P 1:4). Paul insists that the death and resurrection of Christ is an essential part of the mystery of Christ since it was "according to the purpose that God set forth in him" (Eph 1:9). It was only in giving himself to us by emptying himself in his death on the cross (Ph 2:8) that Jesus could reveal the mystery of the depth of God's love for us.

We are God's children and must respond to this great gift and grace with hearts full of gratitude and praise. But we find ourselves inadequate in every way. Again God comes to our rescue, enabling us to praise him as we ought through Christ and the Holy Spirit living within us.

Elements Comprising Paul's Mysterion

We must be cautious in searching for Paul's meaning of the word, *mysterion*, in order not to project into Paul's meaning of our union with Christ and the Trinity our modern understanding of *mysticism*. Mysticism as we generally understand it begins with Pseudo-Dionysius who in his writings attaches to mysticism a specific accent on the more or less ecstatic union of the soul with God.[10] This concept moved far beyond Paul's rich, but more comprehensive understanding of the *mysterion* of Christ in us and we in Christ.

Paul uses this "mystery" as a very fluid reality which helps him to articulate the essence of the mature Christians in a vital, loving relationship with God the Father through Christ and the Holy Spirit. Paul is never concerned with investigating the personal and individual "mystical" states nor to develop the various stages of awareness of Christians that may help them to "be filled with all God's fullness" (Eph 3:19).

Paul wishes to present the whole complex of the Christian life in his preaching and writings as being a vital part of his mystical vision in Christ. The following themes are vital elements in Paul's broad definition of *mysterion*:

justification	suffering, apostolate and
sanctification	eternal glory
faith (*pistis* in Greek)	Christian liberty
initiation rite of Baptism	Agape-love
grace of divine filiation	Christ and the Spirit in us
outpouring of the Holy Spirit	we in Christ and
insertion into the Church	the Holy Spirit
stretching toward perfection	the mystical and
the spiritual combat	the apostolate

---

[10] Joseph Huby, SJ, *Mystiques Paulinienne et Johannique* (Paris: Desclée de Brouwer, 1946).

distrust of self and assurance   communion of Saints.[11]
of salvation

The Revelation of the Mystery

Paul understood that, since Christ is for Christians the fullness of God's revelation of the mystery of salvation, there could be no full mystery before the coming of Christ into our world. The *mysterion* of God's hidden plan of redemption for the human race and the fulfillment of God's entire creation, including the cosmos, was hidden from former ages before Christianity. The prophets of the Old Testament, through God's inspiration, glimpsed the faint outlines of the *mystery* but were able to reveal them to the chosen people only in and through symbols.[12]

Paul makes it clear that such revelation in the "new age," comes about through the Spirit-filled preaching of the "apostles and prophets" (Eph 3:5-6). This would include the twelve apostles, James of Jerusalem and himself. Cerfaux stresses the confidence Paul had that he, the last of all the saints, was granted the grace of preaching to the Gentiles:

> To me, the very least of all the saints, was given the grace of proclaiming to the Gentiles the unfathomable riches of Christ, and to reveal for all the plan of the *mystery* that was hidden for ages in God, the creator of all things, so that the multi-faceted wisdom of God might now be made known through the Church to the rulers and powers in the heavens (Eph 3:8-10).[13]

---

[11] Vladimir Lossky, *Orthodox Theology: An Introduction* (Crestwood, NY: St. Vladimir Seminary Press, 1978), p. 49.

[12] Lucien Cerfaux, *Christ in the Theology of St. Paul* (NY: Herder & Herder, 1962), p. 402 ff.

[13] *Ibid.*, pp. 413-414. On the subject of "principalities," cf. Kittel, ed., *op. cit.*, Vol. I, pp. 74-87.

The Mystery Now Revealed through the Church

A synthesis of Paul's development of the revelation of the *mystery* of Christ would be impossible since he was always growing in his awareness of how Christ is the *mystery* and how he brings knowledge and wisdom of God's salvific plan to the world.

We can see his first development, as Cerfaux points out,[14] coming from his pastoral concerns with the Thessalonian Church. This coincides with the teachings of the apostolic community in Jerusalem and later in the Synoptic Gospels and the Acts of the Apostles. Here we find Paul centering on the eschatological themes of the *parousia* or the second coming of Christ at the end of the world and the resurrection of the dead, as found also developed in 1 Cor 15.

The second stage embraces Paul's deeper growth as reflected in his major epistles, written mainly in his extended ministry in Corinth. As Paul stressed Christ's resurrection and death as the source of new life and power in the lives of Christians, he concentrates on the mystery of God's power and gratuitous generosity now seen in Christ.

The third stage evolved in his letters written during his final captivity in Rome as highlighted in Colossians and Ephesians. In these writings Paul brings together all the elements of Christ the Mystery in his earlier writings, but he develops Christ's resurrectional presence in the world through his Body, the Church. Here we find the greatest witness of Paul to the centrality of Christ as one with the Father and the Spirit in his work to "recapitulate" or return all things to the Father in fulfillment of the Father's salvific plan from all eternity until "...Christ is all and in all" (Col 3:11).

---

[14] *Ibid.*, pp. 529 ff.

Letter to the Colossians

Let us, by way of summary of Paul's central theme of the *mysterion* of God's eternal plan, bring together the fullest development of Paul's theology of Christ, the mystery of our salvation, as found first in Colossians and then in Ephesians.

Paul in Colossians seeks to warn the small band of Christians at Colossae about certain Gnostic teachings, spread most probably by Jewish syncretists who had developed a pseudo-philosophy that endangered the Gospel message by a Gnostic new brand of wisdom opposed to that of God (1 Cor 2:6). Paul also tried to wean the Colossians away from a faulty asceticism which put too much emphasis on the Jewish laws of purification, the avoidance of certain foods and drink, and the heretical practice of worshipping angels.[15]

In responding to the heretical teaching of some Christian Gnostics that made Jesus one of the cosmic luminaries or angels, but not God, Paul gives us a fuller and richer description of Christ our Savior as the center of the entire created universe. He is the Son of God, eternally present in the bosom of the Father, the "first born" of God before any creation. He is pre-eminent in all things. Paul reaches new heights of eloquence as he sings his praises of the cosmic Christ. This is especially evident in Paul's rhapsodic hymn in the first chapter of his letter to the Colossians:

> He is the image of the unseen God,
> the firstborn of all creation.
> For in him all things in heaven and on earth were created,
> both the seen and the unseen...
> All things were created through him
> and for him.

---

[15] Cf. Patrick V. Rogers, CP, *Colossians*, in Series *New Testament Message* 15 (Wilmington, DE: Michael Glazier Inc., 1980), pp. xiii-xvi.

He is before all things,
    and in him all things hold together.
He is the head of the body, the Church...
He is the beginning,
    the firstborn from the dead,
    so that he might be above all else,
For in him all the Fullness was pleased to dwell,
    and through him reconciled all things to himself,
Making peace by the blood of his cross
    reconciling everything on earth
    or in the heavens (Col 1:15-20).

Paul highlights how God has allowed him and the other "saints" to make known "the richness of this glorious mystery among the Gentiles — this *mystery*, which is Christ in you, the hope of glory" (Col 1:27). We, too, come to realize with the early Gentile converts that Christianity is a revealed religion of a unique kind. It was harbored within the Trinity until the coming of Christ, but now in and through the preaching of the Church it has become a truth proclaimed to all peoples. Our hope for eternal life comes about through our personal, experiential contact with Christ who lives in us (2:2-3; 2:6).

By accepting the mystery, the wisdom of Christ, Christians, according to the second part of this epistle (3:1-4, 6) are also to live out the mystery of their Baptism by a mystical death and resurrection into the newness of the life Christ gives to us. "For you have died, and your life is hidden now with Christ in God. When Christ, your life, appears, then you too will appear with him in glory" (3:3-4). Paul indicates the response Christians are to make: to live in Christ in their daily life. The *praxis* of living in the mystery includes renouncing all vices and practicing the virtues of Jesus within the existential situation of one's Christian family and society.

Message to the Ephesians

Following the hypothesis of P. Benoit that the letter to the Ephesians was written after that to the Colossians,[16] we discover in Ephesians a doctrine of universal redemption much more developed and nuanced than in Colossians. Paul seemingly presupposes the universal cosmic primacy of Christ, so strongly insisted on in Colossians, and builds upon it. He writes in a calm, synthetic manner, with none of the polemical overtones so prevalent in Colossians. In Colossians Christ appears in his cosmic role as Head who brings about the perfection or fullness of the cosmic universe, while in Ephesians, Christ is shown to be the mystical Head of the Church.

He brings about the close unity of all believers, both Jews and Gentiles, in himself, by vivifying them with his own life and elevating them to a oneness of Body with him as their Head. In this letter Paul wishes, therefore, to show the Church as the mysterious link between Christ and the cosmos. In Ephesians 1:10, Benoit sees in the *mysterion* of God's will, the union of the Jews and Gentiles in one Body, the Church.[17] Thus Paul would say that God's good will, to gather all human beings into one Body, was "a plan for the fullness of time, to bring all things together in Christ, things in heaven and things on earth" (1:10).

Paul begins this epistle with the fullest expression of the mystery of God's will in creating us human beings to be found in his writings. He situates his readers before the Holy Trinity and calls them to intense humility and gratitude that God has predestined us by having chosen us before the foundation of the world. The mysterious plan of salvation on the part of the Father, Son, and Holy Spirit is that God "chose us in Christ before the foundation of the world to be holy and blameless before

---

[16] P. Benoit, "L'horizon paulinien de l'Epitre aux Ephesians," in *Exegese et Theologie* (Paris, 1961), p. 88.

[17] *Ibid.*, pp. 91-92.

him. In his love he destined us beforehand to be his adopted sons through Jesus Christ, according to the express purpose and desire of his will, to the praise of the glorious grace he bestowed upon us in his beloved" (1:4-6).

The Work of Christ

Paul outlines in summary form the mission of Christ. He offers us redemption by his blood. We receive the forgiveness of our sins through the riches of his grace which he lavishes so generously upon us (Eph 1:7-8). Christ "has made known to us the mystery (*mysterion*) of his [God's] will according to the purpose he displayed in Christ as a plan for the fullness of time — to bring all things together in Christ, things in the heavens and things on earth" (1:9-10).

The Work of the Holy Spirit

It is through the working of the Spirit that Christians have been able to receive the word of truth, "the good news of your salvation" (Eph 1:13) and believe in Jesus as the Son of God from all eternity. It is the work of the Spirit of the risen Lord bestowed upon us in our Baptism to be the seal (in Greek, *sphragis*) or the signature attesting that we belong to Christ through the Spirit promised us by the Son. The Spirit convinces us through his infused gifts of faith, hope and love that, in Baptism, we have "the pledge that we shall gain our inheritance when God redeems what is his, to the praise of his glory" (1:14).

The Mystery of the Church, The Body of Christ

Previously (Eph 1:20-2:10), Paul highlighted Christ's resurrection and exaltation. Now he turns to his death in order to show that Christ is the one who is our Savior and Redeemer by his saving acts. He is now seen as the one who unites what has been separated, breaks down and abolishes obstacles to such unity and brings about the reconciliation of all God's creatures. This is the work of the Church which links Christ with the entire, created cosmos. "This is a tremendous mystery. I am applying it to Christ and the Church" (5:32).

Paul stresses the absolute primacy of Christ over the cosmos as we saw in Colossians and combines it now with the mystical primacy of Christ in his Church. "[God the Father] has put all things under his feet and has given him as head over all things to the Church, which is his body, the fullness of the One who fills all things in their totality" (1:22-23). Christ is absolute Head of the spiritual Body, the Church, whose members have freely, through loving faith, submitted themselves to his absolute primacy.

Paul seeks to describe the bond of union between Christ and the Church by the metaphor of spouses. In this metaphor he strives to convey the duality of dominance and submission through love, and adds the concept of an intimate union resulting in a new life. This is the divine life brought about solely by Christ, the Spouse. Christ is the source of this divine life, not only for his bride, the Church, but also through his activity in the Church for the individual members (5:23-30).

Paul searches for other metaphors and symbols that will convey the mysterious, intimate union of Christ with the individual members in whom he lives by his own divine life. One analogy he uses is that of a building. We members are built up as an edifice upon the foundation of the apostles and prophets "with Christ Jesus himself as the cornerstone.... In him you are being built together into God's dwelling place in the Spirit" (2:20-

22). Without Christ there would be no foundation for this life in the Spirit. Yet the Church has many members with different functions — apostles, prophets, etc. All individual members are distinct from Christ, yet they form one single temple in which God dwells.

Recapitulation in Christ

Paul uses the Greek word, *anakephaloiomai* (Eph 1:9-10) to describe Christ's role assigned in the decree of his heavenly Father, namely, that when the fullness of time had arrived, God would gather all creation, both in heaven and on earth, under the one head, Christ.[18] H. Schlier finds a great variety of possible meanings for this term as it is used in Scripture, but *reestablish* seems to be the best translation.[19] We can accept this to mean that Christ will restore the world's lost unity under his own headship.

Christ at the time of his death and resurrection, in microcosm as it were, reestablished or reconciled humanity in himself by destroying sin, death, and the distorted element in the "flesh." In the second coming, the *parousia*, he will reestablish all things by raising up all of God's creation into a unity into Christ by spiritualizing all. He will bring all things completely under his dominion by bestowing the fullness of his divine life upon human beings for all eternity.

J. Huby has well synthesized how Christ will gather up all things and give them their fullest meaning in himself:

> In him all has been created as in a supreme center of unity, harmony, and cohesion, which gives to the world its sense, its value, and therefore its reality. Or, to use another metaphor, he is the focus, the "meeting point"

---

[18] See Kittel, ed., *op. cit.*, Vol. I, art., *Anakephalaiosis*, by H. Schlier, pp. 673-682.
[19] *Ibid.*

as Lighthouse puts it, where all the fibers and generative energies of the universe are organized and gathered together. Were someone to see the whole universe, past, present and future, in a single instantaneous glimpse, he would see all beings ontologically suspended from Christ, and completely unintelligible apart from him.[20]

Knowledge of the Heart

One last remark must be added that concerns living in active hope and love the mystery of Christ who dwells within our hearts by faith. Paul had often before the writing of Ephesians linked up the *mysterion* with faith and love. In one of his most beautiful prayers Paul prays that his readers have a faith (*pistis* in Greek) that is deeper than a mere assent of the mind. Paul insists that we cannot come to know the mystery of God in Christ by a mere human knowledge (*gnosis*)[21] about Christ and God's redeeming love. Paul instructs the Ephesians that by allowing Christ to live in our hearts through our exercise of faith, hope and love, we open ourselves to a higher knowledge which is beyond any knowledge acquired by our own efforts.

It is the divinely infused wisdom of the Holy Spirit that gives to us an experiential sharing in the fullness of God. His prayer is again centered on the Trinity: Father (3:14), Spirit (3:16), and Christ (3:17).[22]

For this reason I kneel before the Father, from whom every family in heaven and on earth is named, that he may grant you inner strength and power through his Spirit.

---

[20] Joseph Huby, SJ, *Les épitres de la Captivité* (Paris: Beauchesne, 1935), p. 40.

[21] J. Dupont, *Gnosis, La connaissance religieuse dans les épitres de saint Paul* (Louvain, 1949). Also cf. Kittel, ed., *op. cit.*, Vol. I, pp. 689-714.

[22] Cf. Lionel Swain, *Ephesians* in Series *New Testament Message* 13 (Wilmington, DE: Michael Glazier Inc., 1980), pp. 68-69.

May Christ dwell in your hearts through faith, firmly
rooted and established in love, so that with all the saints
you may be able to understand the breadth, the length,
the height, and the depth, and know Christ's love which
surpasses all knowledge so that you may be filled with
all God's fullness (Eph 3:14-19).

Epignosis

Paul uses the Greek word *epignosis* to express a very rich
concept in his theology. Commentators do not always agree
exactly as to any one meaning to this word that Paul uses in
various ways in his writings.[23]

In his letter to the Ephesians Paul uses *epignosis* much as
the Old Testament writers used the Hebrew word *yada*, to
express knowledge not merely of the intellect but of the "heart."
This kind of knowledge gives us not only a noetic understanding about God but empowers the "anawim," the poor in spirit,
to respond to God's call by action.[24] One "knows" the saving
deeds of Yahweh by experiencing his transcendent divinity and
this, in turn, prompts the believer to respond in the way he or
she lives (Dt 4:39; Ps 46:11).

True Christian Wisdom

True Christians possess a wisdom beyond anything they
can acquire by themselves. They "know" certain truths because
God's Spirit breaks into their humble and purified hearts and

---

[23] Cf. Mother Kathryn Sullivan, RSCJ, *"Epignosis" in the Epistles of St. Paul*, in
Studiorum Paulinorum Congressus Internationalis Catholicus 1961, Vol. 2, in
Analecta Biblica, 17-18 (Rome: Pontifical Biblical Institute, 1963), pp. 405-416.
Cf. also Kittel, ed., *op. cit.*, Vol. I, art., *Gnosis*, by R. Bultmann, pp. 703-714.

[24] John L. McKenzie, SJ, *Dictionary of the Bible* (NY: Bruce Publishing Co., 1965);
pp. 486-488. Cf. also, T. Boman, *Hebrew Thought Compared with Greek* (London,
1960), pp. 200-204.

reveals these truths to them by way of *insight*. Revelation, faith, and personal experience all interact to inspire the believer, out of loving obedience, to live according to these truths revealed by Christ. They come to worship God "in spirit and in truth" (Jn 4:23).

Such a knowledge (*epignosis*) brings about a loving communion between friends which embraces the love within the Trinitarian community as well as within the Church, the Body of Christ. This depends upon the degree of self-surrender we give to God's perfect love in the gifts of Jesus Christ and the Holy Spirit as we progressively develop the virtues that evolve in the course of our life "hidden with Christ in God" (Col 3:3).

To know the mystery of Christ in its "breadth and length and height and depth" (Eph 3:18) is not to know any boundaries, but only unbounded riches (Eph 3:8). It means to plunge ever more deeply into the immensity of God's Trinitarian love for each of us as we come to comprehend the Incomprehensible, and stretch out to possess the Unpossessable who makes all other possessions vain (Ph 3:13-14).

Such loving wisdom, Paul insists, is revealed only to those who strive continually to become more holy:

> Yet among the mature we do preach wisdom, but a wisdom which is not of this age nor of the rulers of this age, who are losing their power. Instead we preach God's wisdom, a wisdom which is secret and hidden and which God ordained before the ages for our glory (1 Cor 2:6-7).

Now we are able to turn in the next chapter to discover this true wisdom, taught by Jesus Christ to his first disciples and made available to us, his modern followers, as we explore the riches of St. Paul's phrase, "in Christ" (*en Christo*) which he uses 164 times in his writings.[25]

---

[25] Adolf Deissmann, *Paul: A Study in Social and Religious History*, tr. Wm. E. Wilson (NY: Harper & Bros., 1957), p. 140. Cf. also his classical work, *Die neutestamentliche Formel "in Christo Jesu"* (Marburg, 1892).

2

LIVING "IN CHRIST"

——— ◊ ———

ONE OF THE MOST FREQUENT phrases in St. Paul's writings is the phrase or a variant of it, namely, to *be* or to *live* "in Christ" (*en Christo*, in Greek). It came out of his personal experience of intimate union with the risen Lord Jesus, whom he first encountered on the road to Damascus. This initial experience of the unity of Christ's members really alive in the Lord Jesus, who has conquered sin and death and brought his followers into a new life in Christ, was the key to Paul's theology and his fiery preaching to share that new life in Christ with the Jews and the Gentiles of his day. It was the focal point of his theology of salvation, redemption, and our human sanctification in and through the Spirit of Jesus risen and glorified.

Anthropology offers us through the discovery of human artifacts and crude paintings in places such as the Cro-Magnon caves in Dordogne, France, a consistent history which shows that we human beings have always instinctively sought to find a center around which we could unify the indeterminate, amorphous mass of our daily experiences. Primitive races made this center materially concrete by driving a stake into the earth, thus symbolizing the pinning of a snake's head, a sign of chaos and unreality, to the ground. This spot on the earth gave primitive man an external center for his inner center to relate to, and upon it he built his home.

Later on, primitive races in a hunt, finding a prey and killing it, would signal the place and there they would build a temple to worship their invisible divinity. This would become the center of their social community. Other tribes would often choose a mountain top as the center of their cosmos, and there they would encounter the Supreme Reality of their world.

Christ: The Center for Christians

We Christians do not need to search for the center of our being, the center of our home, the center of our social community, indeed of our cosmos. That center became a reality when the infinitely sacred intersected the finitely profane in the person of Jesus Christ, true God and true man. God, the Supreme Reality, became centered in a humble human body:

> And the Word became flesh
> And dwelt among us,
> And we saw his glory,
> Glory as of the only-begotten of the Father,
> Full of grace and truth (Jn 1:14).

All things came into being through him and without him there is nothing that has existence (Jn 1:3). Paul preached on top of the Areopagus in Athens: "In him we live and move and have our being" (Ac 17:28). This is the vision of Christians of all times. The sacred in the person of Jesus Christ is the center now of the profane, giving it its order, its unity, its fullest reality. Through the profane element of his human body, Jesus Christ has inserted himself into our lives and into the very textural weave of our cosmos. Because that human being died and was raised to a new and glorious life in the resurrection, that sacred center is still inserted into the fabric of our very lives and of our cosmos. He will never cease being our Center.

Still, we not only believe that all reality comes under his dominion, but we also hold by deepest faith that Jesus Christ, through and in his resurrected new life, is working to accomplish the fulfillment of all God's creatures. By an interior force of attraction called love, he is always drawing to himself all human beings, capable of recognizing and acknowledging him as the true Center of their being. Christian faith brings with it the awesome possibility and obligation of building within ourselves a sacred temple, of relating ourselves to this Center, who is the risen Christ, living within us.

Paul saw so clearly in his personal, intimate union with Christ that Christ permeates and leavens the profane world of "the flesh and the devil" until "When everything is made subject to him, then the Son himself will be subjected to the One who subjected everything to the Son, so that God will be all in all" (1 Cor 15:28; cf. Col 3:11; Eph 4:6). It is Christ who is before all things and in whom everything is held together (cf. Col 1:17). Paul, more than any other sacred writer, beheld Christ immersed in and energizing the created, material world.

In Paul's captivity letters, especially Colossians and Ephesians, Christ is shown as the center of unity for all that has been created. Paul would wish to lead us high up on the mountain of faith to gaze out upon the whole universe. If we share his faith, we shall see Christ as the Center and focal point toward whom and from whom all things flow, verifying Heidegger's insight that truth is ultimately full reality. All beings have their ontological intelligibility and are "true" to the degree that their relationship "in being" to Ultimate Reality is comprehended.

Edward Schillebeeckx expresses this truth even more clearly:

> In Christ, and through him, human existence has become the objective expression of God's absolute communication of himself to man, and by the same token, the objective expression of the human response to that total

divine gift.... This also reveals the fact that thanks to Christ all of human history is swathed in God's love; it is assumed into the absolute and gratuitous presence of the mystery of God. The worldly and the temporal remain worldly and temporal; they are not sacralized, but sanctified by that presence, that is, by the God-centered life of Christ and of his faithful.[1]

Dynamic Growth in Christ

One of Paul's original theological contributions to the early Church was his doctrine of the dynamic growth of the individual Christian, the Church, and the cosmos "in Christ." On these three planes he viewed Christ's incarnation as being prolonged in space and time and eventually touching all creatures. Yet he never separated these three areas from one another. An individual Christian, who is growing in Christ, is helping to build up the full Body of Christ, the Church, which, as a leaven, is moving the universe closer to its completion in Christ Jesus. Then "Christ is all and in all" (Col 3:11).

Fernand Prat, S.J., in his two-volume work on *The Theology of St. Paul*, points out how the phrase, *in Christ*, is often used by Paul and rarely if ever found in the other New Testament writers:

The formula is as common in St. Paul as it is rare elsewhere. It recurs in all his Epistles except in the one to Titus.... However, it is not everywhere distributed equally. As one might have anticipated, it is much more frequent in the Epistles of the captivity, the principal subject of which is the mystical union of Christians with Christ.[2]

---

[1] E. Schillebeeckx, ed., *The Church and Mankind* in series *Concilium*, Vol. 1 (NY: Paulist Press, 1964), pp. 81-82.

[2] Fernand Prat, SJ, *The Theology of St. Paul*, Vol. 2; tr. John L. Stodder (Westminster, MD: The Newman Bookshop, 1958), p. 391.

It was Adolf Deissmann, a Protestant scholar on the writings of St. Paul, who first published a comprehensive work on the phrase "in Christ" in 1892.[3] He had discovered 164 texts in the writings of Paul which use the formula "in Christ" or its equivalent expression as "in Christ Jesus" or "in the Lord" (*Kyrio*). Deissmann was a strong advocate that the formula, "in Christ" was used by Paul to express the most intimate union possible between the Christian and Christ, the resurrected, spiritual Lord of the universe. In a word, Deissmann calls Paul's mystical vision a "Christ-mysticism."[4]

Meaning of the Phrase, In Christ

Deissmann in his detailed research on the two words of this special formula of Paul has insisted that the first part, the preposition, *en*, must in the majority of cases with the dative case in Greek, *Christo*, always imply a "local" sense that for Paul would denote a mystical relationship between the Christian individual and Christ. The phrase occurs in the most diverse contexts, but in every case it refers to a state of mystical union, of *being* in Christ.[5]

---

[3] A. Deissmann, *Die neutestamentliche Formel "in Christo Jesus"* (Marburg, 1892). Cf. his other work in English, *Paul: A Study in Social and Religious History*, tr. William E. Wilson (NY: Harper & Bros. Publishers, 1957).

[4] Deissmann, *Paul, op. cit.*, p. 147.

[5] *Ibid.*, p. 152. For some of the leading scholars and their research on the meaning of the formula, *en Christo*, cf. Dom François Gerritzen, OSB, *"Le Sens et L'Origine de L'En Christo Paulinien"* in *Studiorum Paulinorum Congressus Internationalis Catholicus* (1961) in series *Analecta Biblica* (1718), Vol. 2 (Rome: Pontifical Biblical Institute, 1963), pp. 323-331.

J. Huby, *Mystiques Paulinienne...*, *op. cit.*, pp. 13 ff.; E. Mocsy, "De unione mystica cum Christo" in *Verbum Domini*, Vol. 25 (1947), pp. 270-279, 328-339; F. Prat, *op. cit.*, note M, pp. 391-395; Kittel, ed., *op. cit.*, Vol. II, art., *En*, by A. Oepke, pp. 537-543; H.E. Weber, "Die Formel 'in Christo' und die paulinische Christusmystik" in *Neue kirchliche Zeitschrift*, Vol. 31 (1920), pp. 213-260; M.R. Weijers, *"In Christo-Jesu"* in *Revue Thomiste*, Vol. 47 (1947), pp. 499-516; A. Wikenhauser, *op. cit.*, pp. 21-108.

Deissmann calls Paul a communion-mystic. He describes this intimate union with Christ within Paul and all fervent Christians who live "in Christ" this way:

> In communion with Christ he (Paul) found communion with God; Christ-intimacy was the experience and confirmation of God-intimacy. He was not deified nor was he transformed into spirit by this communion, nor did he become Christ.... But he was transformed by God, he became spiritual and he was one whom Christ possessed (Gal 3:29) and a Christ-bearer.[6]

There are many texts where Paul uses the usual formula, *in Christ*, without any true reference to the mystical union between the Christian and the risen Lord Jesus. But as we are concerned primarily with Paul's mystical vision, let us look at the many nuances he brings to the same formula when he is thinking of the indwelling presence of Christ living within the Christian and the Christian living in the resurrected Lord.

Mystical Realism of Being in Christ

Paul's realism quickens our faith that was given to us in our Baptism enabling us to realize that we have been "incorporated" or inserted into the very life of the risen Savior and now with Christ in us we are made into a "new creation" (2 Cor 5:17). Baptism gives us direct contact with the resurrected, glorified Christ who now, in his spiritualized Body, truly dwells within us. Christ has become our reconciliation with God, and so "...we boast of God through our Lord Jesus Christ, through whom we have now received reconciliation" (Rm 5:11).

Through his Holy Spirit Christ brings about the discarding of the "old man" in order that we might live in Christ ac-

---

[6] Deissmann, *Paul...*, pp. 152-153.

cording to the "new man." The "new man" is precisely the given individual, baptized in Christ, now living according to this new inner principle of life that is Christ. Once we begin to live out our baptism by dying to self, having been crucified with Christ, we find that we live, no longer we ourselves, but Christ lives in us. "I live by faith in the Son of God who has loved me and given himself up for me" (Gal 2:19-20).

This new life, through our union with Christ, makes us sons and daughters of God (Gal 3:26), alive unto God (Rm 6:11), called *saints* (Ph 1:1; 4:21), sanctified (1 Cor 1:2) and now we enjoy access to the heavenly Father (Eph 3:12). There can be no more condemnation "for those who are in Christ Jesus" (Rm 8:1).

This mystical union in Christ brings us into God's redeeming justification. Paul writes: "For our sake God had Christ become sin, even though he was without sin, so that in Christ we might become the righteousness of God" (2 Cor 5:21). When, in the "old man," we were dead because of our transgressions and sins according to the "flesh" (*sarx*), God, so rich in his mercy, "brought us to life together with Christ — you've been saved by grace — he raised us up with him, and had us sit together with Christ in the heavenly realms" (Eph 2:4-7).

Living in the risen Christ, we baptized Christians have new powers. We have become adopted children of God (Gal 4:5; 3:26) and are aware through the Holy Spirit that we live in a relationship similar to that which exists between God the Father and his only begotten Son, Jesus Christ, because we now have the same life of the Son within us. In Baptism we become like Christ. We can call the Father, *Abba*, and know we really are "children of God, and if we're children then we're also heirs, heirs of God and co-heirs with Christ, if only we suffer with him so as to be glorified with him as well" (Rm 8:17).

Christ Living in Us

Christ lives in us and shares with us his very life as both
God and man in an ongoing synergism. In him we can do all
things; without him we can do nothing. This combination of
divine grace and human cooperation can effect things otherwise impossible. Thus for Paul the two formulas go together
since they speak of the *I-Thou* relationship between Christ and
ourselves.[7]

In Chapter One we cited Paul's clear statement: "But now
it has been revealed to his saints, to whom God chose to make
known the richness of this glorious mystery among the Gentiles; this mystery is *Christ in you*, the hope of glory" (Col 1:26-
27). Paul uses the phrase "in Christ" to express the real union
between us and the indwelling Christ in the ontological order.
He uses the phrase "Christ in us" to stress the active presence
of the risen Lord and Savior in us. It is through grace that we
are able to say with St. Paul, "It is no longer I who live, it is
Christ who lives in me!" (Gal 2:20); and it is through our cooperation and the working of Christ's Spirit-filled presence within
us that we can live his life anew in our own daily lives. Christ
in us is the new Adam, "a life-giving spirit" (1 Cor 15:45).

St. Paul doesn't write a lot about Christ indwelling us, for
he knows that we come to this realization only in and through
the Holy Spirit whose principal work in our sanctification is to
gift us with the knowledge of Christ in us — a knowledge, as
he says, that surpasses all understanding (Eph 3:18-19). When
Paul speaks of Christ Jesus dwelling in himself and in other
individual Christians (2 Cor 13:3), he usually does so in connection with his dwelling in the community of Christians. Paul
talks about Christ being formed in us in order to build up the
body of Christ when he speaks of being "in labor" a second
time. Some of his community had fallen away from their ear-

---

[7] Cf. Wikenhauser, pp. 40-48.

lier fervor and now Paul writes to them: "My children, once again I'm suffering birth pains until Christ takes form in you" (Gal 4:19). His work is to bring forth Christ in them so that Christ may be imaged in their daily life of piety and conduct as the new People of God. Some of this is seen in his strong reprimand to the Christians of Corinth: "Do you not realize that Jesus Christ is in you? — Or have you failed the test?" (2 Cor 13:5).

Putting on Christ

Another expression used by Paul to indicate his understanding of the term living "in Christ," is his phrase: "putting on Christ." We see Paul using this metaphor to suggest that those baptized in Christ are enveloped by the person and power of the indwelling Christ, wrapped up in him as in a heavenly robe.

We see this metaphor used a few times, e.g., Gal 3:27-29; 1 Cor 12:13 and Col 3:11. All three texts imply the same truth that to become truly a mature Christian one must begin by actualizing his or her "incorporation into Christ" through Baptism. The clearest reference to Baptism and the putting on of Christ is found in Gal 3:27: "For all of you who were baptized into Christ have clothed yourselves with Christ." Carolyn Osiek, R.S.C.J. in her commentary on Galatians explains the relation of putting on Christ and the putting on of the baptismal robe: "Though such a practice is definitely attested only much later, this expression may already refer to the custom of removing one's clothes before immersion in the baptismal water and putting on a new white garment after ascending from the pool (see Rm 14:13; Eph 4:24)."[8]

Thus we see that Paul used a variety of formulas to express his most frequently used phrase "in Christ." Commentators of Paul's writings have long discussed his special use of *in*

---

[8] Carolyn Osiek, RSCJ, *Galatians* (Wilmington, DE: Michael Glazier, 1980), Message 12, pp. 39-40.

Christ and *in the Spirit.* It is important to see how Paul himself uses these two phrases since he never could conceive the risen Lord Jesus without the operations of the Holy Spirit giving us power "to know him (Jesus Christ) and the power of his resurrection, to understand the fellowship of his sufferings and become conformed to his death, in the hope of somehow attaining resurrection from the dead" (Ph 3:10-11).

H. Gunkel has studied the interrelationships in these two Pauline phrases.[9] He emphasizes the close and constant relations which exist between the phrases, *en Christo* and *en pneumati* (the Holy Spirit). He concludes with the summation: "All the operations of the *pneuma* (the Spirit) appear in other places as operations of Christ."[10] We shall develop this in another chapter that will focus exclusively on the workings of the Holy Spirit.

If we follow F. Prat's advice,[11] we could work our way through a concordance and see how many times we find the phrase, *en Christo,* and try to replace it by the phrase, *en pneumati.* What we would find is that both of these phrases can be interchanged without too much altering of the intended sense by Paul. The exceptions to this statement would be those references to *in Christ* that apply to God's predestination of us in the God-man incarnate or when the phrase applies specifically to the historical Jesus Christ as the second Adam. We need also to exclude the references, *in the Spirit,* that refer specifically to the Holy Spirit, such as the *charismata* of the Holy Spirit.

Prat wisely points out: "That even where the substitution is absolutely possible, it almost always causes the loss of a very delicate shade of meaning, like that which would be produced by putting soul instead of head, or *vice versa,* in the description of the mystical body."[12]

---

[9] H. Gunkel, *Die Wirkungen des Heiligen Geistes* (Göttingen, 1909, 3rd ed.)
[10] *Ibid.,* p. 97.
[11] F. Prat, *op. cit.,* p. 394.
[12] *Ibid.*

Growth in Christ

By way of summary of the richness contained in Paul's phrase *in Christ*, we must understand that our new life in Christ must grow as an embryo grows in the womb. Paul wanted to spend himself in order that his Christian converts might grow up into Christ, "... until Christ takes form in you" (Gal 4:19). Christ's life within us admits of growth, dependent on our co-operation with God's grace. From the embryonic life given to us in Baptism, we are to progress "to mature manhood, to the extent of Christ's full stature" (Eph 4:13).

Again Paul shows this growth as a progress in unity of faith and deeper knowledge of the Son of God whereby "with all the saints you may be able to understand the breadth, the length, the height, and the depth, and know Christ's love which surpasses all knowledge so that you may be filled with all God's fullness" (Eph 3:18-19). The effect of this real union with Christ is the activation in an individual's life of Christlike piety and conduct. We Christians are raised to a new life by possessing a new principle of activity, Christ himself. But we are also to "walk in the newness of life" (Rm 6:4) as we live *in Christ*.

Already and Not Yet

In the process of growing into Christ we are in a sense what we are growing to be. We can speak of our having already attained the goal because we shall attain it if we live constantly in greater union with Christ, our total strength in whom we can do all things (2 Cor 12:9-10). Our nature is perfected because we are always stretching out toward the goal (Ph 3:10-11) by daily putting off sin in our lives as we fight evil tendencies. In this sense *in Christ* gives us the inner power to surely arrive in the life to come to be *with Christ*, in the eschatological sense of eternal glorious life as children of God and heirs with him of Heaven forever (Rm 8:17).

Thus Paul, depending on his view of the growth process which is defined by its goal, can say that we have been saved (Eph 2:5, 8), for God cannot do more in showing his love and mercy for us than by giving us his divine Son to die that we might inherit a sharing in God's very own nature (2 P 1:4). Still from our side of the relationship in view of the dynamic, ongoing process toward the final goal and the many obstacles of sinfulness within us and around us, he can say that we are "in the process of being saved" (1 Cor 1:18; 2 Cor 2:15). Hence the Christian life in Christ is precisely a continuous process of ridding ourselves of all self love, of casting off the "outward person" in order to renew constantly the "inward person" (2 Cor 4:16) so as to grow into the fullness of Christ. And above all it is important, in speaking of this reality, that we Christians ever keep in mind the intimate, loving relationship we have between ourselves living in Christ's new life.

3

UNION WITH CHRIST

———— ◊ ————

THE END OF OUR HUMAN existence is to live in the intimacy of the divine Trinity's love and to grow evermore in deeper union with God. "God is love," writes John (1 Jn 4:8). This means that God is always an intimate presence of total availability in the sharing of his divine life with us. But how are we to attain such intimacy with God if we treat God as absent in our lives? The "mystery" of God's eternal plan for us and his created world and the proof of God's passionate love for each of us is, in Paul's words, "the mystery of Jesus Christ." By the Holy Spirit's gifts of faith, hope and love infused into us in our Baptism and intensified by our continued cooperation with God's grace, we can come to new knowledge beyond our understanding (Eph 3:17-18) and wisdom to enter into God's reality.

This reality unfolds for us in our faith. We believe that Jesus Christ, the historical person who lived in historical time, on our planet, born of a human mother, is "one with God from all eternity" (Ph 2:6). He "did not consider equality with God something to hold on to. Instead, he emptied himself and took on the form of a slave, born in human likeness.... He humbled himself and became obedient, even unto death, death on a cross" (Ph 2:7-8).

Now we can have certitude beyond our own reasoning that as the Father loves him, so he, Jesus Christ, loves us (Jn 15:9). Let us now examine how Paul in various ways describes this intimate, loving union of Christ and ourselves. We can understand with our limited head-knowledge the truth of God's omnipresence (Rm 1:19-21). Yet, even for the average Christian, God, who is "everywhere," is really "nowhere."

God is present in a special way in Heaven. Yet for most of us Heaven is conceived as a "space up there," far away, nebulous and not very present to us who live, not there, but here on planet Earth. We believe by our Christian faith that Jesus Christ is present to us in the Eucharist. In this sacrament we can "take and eat and drink" of the Body and Blood of Christ. In a mysterious way we believe we are in a loving union with Christ, but this presence fades as we go forth from our eucharistic celebration when "the Mass is ended."

Thus most of us never live a life of intimacy with Jesus Christ throughout each day, as we face our daily problems alone. We are not guided by the immanent indwelling presence of Christ in us as Paul so zealously wanted all human beings to do. Paul himself was vitally aware of his union with Christ, living in him, and he with great zeal wanted all other human beings, "Jews and Gentiles," to experience what was so real to him. "It is no longer I who live, it's Christ who lives in me! And this life I live now in the flesh, I live through faith in the Son of God, who loved me and gave himself up for me" (Gal 2:20).

We have already seen in Chapter Two that Paul was convinced that every Christian through Baptism is joined in a mystical union with Christ risen. This is what Paul signifies by his favorite and unique formula, to live *in Christ.* Now let us search through Paul's writings to understand the true nature of this union with Christ as Paul had received it directly from the Lord himself. "For I did not receive it from a human being, nor was I taught it — I received it through a revelation of Jesus Christ" (Gal 1:12).

God's Constant and Perfect Love for Us

To understand the mystery of our union with Christ dwelling within us, we must keep in mind the context in which Paul wrote (or dictated) his epistles. We have already seen various formulas used by Paul to express this mysterious union with Christ. But it is chiefly Paul's favorite and most frequently used phrase, *in Christ*, that he uses to express the new life that the glorified Christ brings to Christians. By this union Paul means more than a moral oneness in fellowship with the Lord, who sits in glory at the right hand of the Father.

Paul never conceives Christ Jesus in us in a material manner, a concrete, physical way of existing within us. He, in so many ways, leads us into the indwelling presence of Christ Jesus by maintaining always the "mystery" of God's perfect love for us and our return of that love to God in and through Christ and the Holy Spirit. If we wish to enter into Paul's mystical vision of our unity in love with the risen Lord, we must strenuously avoid any "objectification" of Christ's union within us. Paul insists that our experience of this intimate union must always be based upon the Good News of the Triune God's great love for us when we were created by God "according to the image and likeness" that is Jesus Christ (Gn 1:26-27).

We cannot be satisfied with a mere catalogue of Pauline texts that a grammarian might collect to describe this indwelling union with the risen Lord. We must reject any non-mystical, non-faith approach such as A. Deissmann proposed when he removed the mystical, faith roots of Paul's vision by relegating the form of our union with Christ in us as something like the air that surrounds us. In his explanation of our intimate union in Christ, Deissmann correctly writes that Paul avoids any philosophical and binding, intellectual limitations in his attempts to explain how Christ indwells us in the fullness of his historical personhood as God-Man. He writes:

The Apostle remains (in his writings) popular, and in ancient style, vivid in his formulation. He probably thought of some light, ethereal form of existence, such as he doubtless attributed to God.[1]

We see a failure in Deissmann's approach whereby he wishes to avoid any "sarkic" or "flesh" concept in presenting Christ as the risen, spiritual person in all the fullness of his new life dwelling within us. To imagine Christ risen and dwelling within us with a spiritual, ethereal *body* is for Deissmann to remove himself from the world of Paul's mystical vision and to continue to materialize Christ's presence within us.

The Flesh and Body in the New Testament

If we are to enter into Paul's vision of our new relationship with God, we must understand carefully the meaning of *flesh* and *body* as used in the New Testament, especially in Paul's writings.[2] As for the Old Testament writers and those of the New Testament, body (*soma* in Greek) does not refer to a separable component of our make-up as human beings, but rather points to the whole human person in his or her potential for action in the temporal world. We not only *have* a body, but we *are embodied* beings. As such we make choices for our actions in obedience or disobedience to God's will.

Paul seeks to describe the whole person when he refers to human beings as "flesh" (*sarx*). We are considered as whole, embodied persons in respect to our human existence. *Sarx* represents for Paul the human person in all its creaturehood in contrast to God. The "body" or the "flesh" is for Paul what constitutes human persons, not only in their distance and differ-

---

[1] Deissmann, *Paul...*, *op. cit.*, p. 142.
[2] Cf. C.A. Van Peursen, *Body, Soul, Spirit: A Survey of the Body-Mind Problem* (London: Oxford Univ. Press, 1966).

ence from God in their mortality and weakness, but also in their utter estrangement from God through sin. "All have sinned and, therefore, are deprived of God's glory" (Rm 3:23).

Paul shows the "flesh" as the seat of all passionate desires, set awry as long as a person does not ascend and put on the "spirit of Christ." The *flesh* element is not sinful by its nature, but in fact it does open the door to sin through inordinate self-love.

Christ the Redeemer

It is in the light, therefore, of the flesh-spirit antithesis that Paul highlights the saving, healing power of Jesus Christ as Redeemer. Through the incarnation, the Son of God broke through the barrier separating the realm of divinity and true life from that of humanity and death, both physical and moral. Although personally sinless, Christ came "in the likeness of sinful flesh and as an offering for sin, he condemned sin in the flesh" (Rm 8:3). Christ entered a humanity in a state of "unsalvation" which bore the sign of sin, namely, death (Rm 5:12).

By his death and resurrection, Jesus passes from the state of flesh (*sarx*) according to Paul's teaching, to enter into that of the spirit (*pneuma*). As long as Jesus was confined, as we are, to his human flesh, he was not able to share his divine life with other human beings. But after his glorious resurrection, he, "the last Adam (became) a life-giving spirit" (1 Cor 15:45).

Christ first experiences the effects of redemption within his own flesh. He conquers death by the transforming glory of his resurrection in which his carnal condition, that is, the state of estrangement from God, is transformed into the fullness of the Spirit of God's life. Just as his humanity was an integral part of his way of touching human beings, so now, by his resurrection the entire "embodied" person of Christ can touch the embodied personhood of all human beings and through such "divinized" children of God, the whole universe can receive a new orientation toward God. The glorified bodiliness of Jesus becomes, through the working of his Holy Spirit, the source of eternal life for all who believe, for "if the Spirit of God who raised Christ from the dead dwells within you, then the One who raised Christ from the dead will give life to your dead bodies through his Spirit that dwells within you" (Rm 8:11).

The Resurrection and Union with Christ

It was Paul who developed the importance of faith in the risen Lord as the foundation for our Christian life in Christ and his life in us. We are led into the mystery of Christ that is rooted in the heart of all reality, namely, God is love (1 Jn 4:8). Experience teaches us that when persons are in love, they enter into a relationship which does not negate but rather enhances the very uniqueness of each person involved. Dying to self, like seed in fertile soil, they rise to a new and more glorious life born of their union with one another in love.

The experience of resurrection is at the source of all reality. It is love moving out of self-controlled reason to trustful abandonment. When we take the risk we will discover that, in losing our life, we find it in greater abundance. Paul in all his writings saw our mystical union with Christ as grounded on this essential doctrine of Christianity.

The Centrality of Christ's Resurrection

We cannot experience intimate union in Christ without believing in Christ's resurrection and experiencing something of the eternal which makes our union with him as the gloriously risen and victorious Lord of the universe possible *now*. Before Christ's resurrection, he was limited as we are in finite time and space. But by his resurrection he is able to transcend the limitations of time and space to indwell in deepest intimacy with Christians all over the earth in every age.

The resurrection of Christ for Paul is not only pivotal to the life and mission of Jesus; it is fundamental to God's eternal plan of salvation. That is why Paul saw so clearly the centrality of Jesus' resurrection, for "… if Christ wasn't raised, our faith is worthless and you are still in your sins" (1 Cor 15:17). The Pauline scholar, Ernst Käsemann, summarized the glory of Jesus in his resurrection as his ability to lead his disciples on earth to share in the process of his death and resurrection:

> For Paul the glory of Jesus consists in the fact that he makes his disciples on earth willing and able to bear the cross after him, and the glory of the Church and of Christian life consists in the fact that they have the honor of glorifying the crucified Christ as the wisdom and power of God, to seek salvation in him alone, and to let their lives become a service to God under the sign of Golgotha. The theology of the resurrection is at this point a chapter in the theology of the cross, not its supersession.[3]

To Know Christ and the Power of His Resurrection

In a way Jesus is the same person in the resurrection as he was before his death. Yet in a very real sense he is totally different: "I am the first and the last, I am he who lives. I was dead, but now I live forever and ever, and I hold the keys to death and of death's realm" (Rv 1:18). We are in need of receiving from God's Spirit a new knowledge that is experiential. Paul made this his constant prayer for himself and his early Christian converts:

---

[3] Ernst Käsemann, "The Pauline Theology of the Cross" in *Interpretation*, Vol. 24, no. 2, p. 177; cited by Lloyd Geering, *Resurrection: A Symbol of Hope* (London: Hodder & Stoughton, 1971), p. 225.

> ... to know him and the power of his resurrection, to
> understand the fellowship of his sufferings and become
> conformed to his death, in the hope of somehow attain-
> ing resurrection from the dead (Ph 3:10-11).

A Growth Process that Knows No End

This growth in knowledge of the risen Lord is a process
that knows no end. It embodies some of the paradoxes of our
life: Lose your life and you will find it. Death is resurrection. It
is in giving that we receive, in pardoning that we are pardoned
and in *dying that we are born to eternal life.* Love is suffering,
but it is also joy. It unites but also heightens distinctions. The
words of Teilhard de Chardin: "Love differentiates as it unites,"
capture well Paul's understanding of how the mystery of Christ's
resurrection makes it possible for us to live in the power of
Christ's Holy Spirit. The Spirit brings all things into a oneness
in Christ in his Mystical Body, the Church, while developing
the uniqueness of each human person living in Christ as a sin-
gular participation of God's infinite beauty and perfect love.

Living in a New Time

Jesus risen lives outside of time in what Paul calls the
kairos, or the salvific moment which we enter into when,
through Baptism, we participate in Christ's victory over sin and
death and are healed of our death-dealing isolation and self-
centeredness.[4] We meet the risen Lord in the *now,* where salvific
time, the *kairos,* intersects the *chronos* or our historical, pass-
ing time. That is why for Paul we cannot consider Christ's res-

---

[4] For a complete treatment of the meaning of *kairos,* cf. Kittel, ed., *op. cit.,* Vol. III,
art., *Kairos,* by G. Delling, pp. 455-464.

urrectional apparitions as historical happenings alone. Men and women in the New Testament witness to their encounter with the risen Jesus as faith experiences.

Jesus risen had sent them the vivifying Spirit to lead them into the *now* experience of his indwelling presence. Jesus thus enabled them to participate, even in their earthly life, in his own resurrected eternal life. Into our brokenness Jesus comes with the Father to lift us up and, in his Spirit, he gives us a share in his divine life of love.

A New Presence

After his resurrection, Jesus accommodated himself to his followers by assuming a form in which they could still recognize him. He also pushed them to "see" him with the eyes of faith, as Jesus in his resurrectional apparition told the doubting Thomas: "... be not unbelieving, but believe.... Blessed are those who have not seen yet have believed" (Jn 20:27, 29). To meet Jesus as the new creation, the Second Adam, his disciples needed, and we ourselves also need, to make the step gradually from the historical, "physical" Jesus to the risen Lord. Thus those eyewitnesses had a direct and personal experience of an "embodied" Jesus. It was the same Jesus of Nazareth, but now he is present to his believers in a new way. The Holy Spirit gave them the power to recognize him through an experiential knowledge of his presence. In time they would no longer need to "see"; they would "know" that he was near, indeed that he dwelt within them. Jesus risen would give them the power to witness to others so they too would be able to "know," as John writes:

> Whoever keeps his commandments remains in God, and God remains in him. And this is how we know that he remains in us — from the Spirit that he gave us (1 Jn 3:24).

The Victory of the Risen Lord

The good news that pervades every page of the New Testament is that Jesus has died for love of us, but is now risen and lives in us so that we, too, need never live again under the bondage of sin and death. We are capable of entering into his glorious, eternal life by confessing our sins and living only for him as our Lord. He is the first fruits of the new creation (2 Cor 5:17). He is the new Adam who brings us in Baptism a rebirth to new life through his Holy Spirit. Thus Paul writes to Titus:

> But when the goodness and loving kindness of God our Savior appeared — not because of any righteous deeds we had performed, but through his mercy — he saved us through the bath of rebirth and renewal in the Holy Spirit which he poured out upon us so richly through our Savior Jesus Christ in order that we might be restored to fellowship with God by his grace and become heirs in hope of eternal life (Tt 3:4-7).

The Saving Power of the Holy Spirit

The power of the Holy Spirit in Paul's thinking and writing can never be separated from the risen Lord Jesus. Although Paul always maintains the uniqueness of each distinct person in the Blessed Trinity, the Spirit and the risen Lord are for him, as St. Irenaeus in the 2nd century wrote, "the two hands of God come to bring us salvation."[5] It is only through the Spirit of God's love for us that we can believe and experience in our lives that Jesus is truly God-Man, the *Kyrios*, the *Pantokrator*, the Almighty Redeemer and Savior who lives in us. "And no one can say,

---

[5] Irenaeus, *Adversus Haereses*, abbrev. *A.H.*, V, 6, p. 531 in series *The Ante-Nicene Fathers*, Vol. I, ed. A. Roberts and J. Donaldson (Grand Rapids, MI: Eerdmans, 1962).

'Jesus is Lord,' except under the influence of the Holy Spirit" (1 Cor 12:3; 1 Jn 3:24).[6]

We shall develop Paul's theology of the Holy Spirit in another chapter since the Spirit is seen as a distinct power from the power of the risen Jesus. Yet he is inseparable from the risen Lord. The Spirit is presented to us in Pauline writings as the new way of existing and acting by the risen Jesus. He is Christ's life-giving Spirit to the world. He draws us into union with Christ, into his Body, the Church. The Spirit divinizes us, making us true children of God (Rm 8:15; Gal 4:6) and new creatures in Christ Jesus (2 Cor 5:17). The Spirit is not an intermediary between Christ and ourselves. The Spirit and Christ are distinct persons of the Trinity, dwelling within us, distinct in the mode of their actions.[7]

Union with the Father through the Spirit and Son

Paul never denies that our union with Christ and the Spirit brings us into union with the heavenly Father. Yet he does not highlight this as the Johannine writings do. Rather he focuses primarily on our union with the risen Christ and on our manifestation of the new creation in our daily lives through the Holy Spirit. Yet he clearly points out that *in Christ* we have access to the Father (Eph 3:12). If we are united with Christ, then we belong to the Father as Jesus belongs to the Father. We are heirs of Heaven and coheirs with Christ forever of the Trinitarian life, because God has raised us up with him and "seated us together with Christ in the heavenly realms" (Eph 2:6).

St. Augustine well describes our union with the Father if we are also united with the Son and Holy Spirit: "In loving Christ you love the Son of God. In loving the Son of God, you love

---

[6] For Paul's meaning of *Kyrios*, cf. Kittel, ed., *op. cit.*, Vol. III, art., *Kyrios*, by G. Quell, pp. 1039-1081.

[7] J. Huby, *Mystiques Paulienne...*, *op. cit.*, pp. 88-91.

also the Father. It is impossible to divide divine love."[8] The same applies to the Holy Spirit. If the Spirit dwells in us and is with the Son, so the Spirit and the Son and the heavenly Father also dwell in us.

Christ Sits at the Right Hand of the Father

Wikenhauser presents us with Paul's seeming paradox that Christ as risen Lord sits at the right hand of the Father and yet also Christ lives in his Christian followers (2 Cor 5:17) and offers us a solution to the seeming dilemma:

> But they are not incompatible. The idea of the Spirit provides the link between the two. Because of his spiritual existence Christ can sit at the right hand of the Father in Heaven, while simultaneously abiding and working in Christians on earth. The difficulty in understanding this is lessened if we recall that we are not speaking of Christ's physical location when we say that he sits at the right hand of the Father. This expression denotes his divinity; it means that he is raised above the limitations of humanity, and that his Being and operation are divine.
>
> On the other hand... when we speak of Christ's indwelling we refer to the significance of the spiritual Christ for the interior life of Christians on earth.[9]

Summary of Our Union with Christ

1. We have seen an array of phrases to describe the one and same union between us Christians and Christ. This union means always the living and loving relationship from the side of Christ risen who abides in us in the fullness of his love. From

---

[8] St. Augustine, *In Epist. 1 Joan. X*, n. 3, *P.L.*, Vol. 35; ed. Migne; p. 2055.
[9] Wikenhauser, pp. 89-90.

our side of the relationship we live *in Christ* and we can grow progressively in greater unity with Christ as we cooperate with God's grace.

2. Because this union, brought about by the divinizing power of the Holy Spirit, is a living intimacy between Christ and ourselves, it admits of an ever-increasing growth in faith, hope and love: "Put off the old man, your former way of life which is corrupted by deceitful desires! Be renewed in your mind and spirit and put on the new man created in accordance with God's design in true righteousness and holiness" (Eph 4:22-24).

Paul tells the Philippians what he does, and what all Christians should do also, in this growing union with Christ. He considers all other things a loss or "so much rubbish" in comparison with his desire to gain Christ (Ph 3:8-9). He knows he lives in Christ, but he also realizes that there is still "sin" in his members (Rm 7:20-23). And for this reason he continues his pursuit "in the hope of making it [knowledge of Christ and resurrection from the dead] my own, because Christ Jesus has made me his own" (Ph 3:12).

3. Paul sees our union with the indwelling Christ as a real, objective state. He always experienced in his lifetime on earth the total, risen Jesus Christ and this is the experience that he preached.

4. However this union of a Christian and Christ does not mean for Paul that it is a substantial union which results in one person who remains, Jesus Christ, through an absorption of our unique individual existence. Wikenhauser cites B. Bartmann[10] insisting that through our union with Christ the new creation of 2 Cor 5:17 "makes a physical change in our spirit and its capacities, and the new life which we receive is something real. But this physical change is not substantial. It is merely acci-

---

[10] B. Bartmann, *Die Grundzuge seiner Lehre und die moderne Religionsgeschichte* (Paderborn, 1914), p. 118.

dental, and so it does not produce an indelible natural effect. Its effect is in the order of grace, and it may be undone."[11]

5. This intimate union between ourselves and Christ is a mutual presence, a compenetration, a reciprocal unity and a mutual sharing of each other in self-sacrificing love. "… you are all one in Christ Jesus. And if you belong to Christ, then you're Abraham's descendants, heirs in accordance with the promise" (Gal 3:28-29).

6. Paul's mystical union between Christ and ourselves can never be a static relationship. He never sees the individual reaching a point of perfect union with Christ that will enable him to cease from "stretching" forward (*epekteinomenos*, in Greek, one who "strains forward as a runner in a stadium"). "I don't consider that I've won yet, and for this reason I forget what's behind me and reach out for what's in front of me. I strain toward the goal to win the prize of God's heavenward call in Christ Jesus" (Ph 3:13-14).

7. Paul never holds out as the fruit and goal of our union with Christ any ecstatic feeling of losing one's selfhood to be forever transformed into divinity. In the process of being divinized through the Spirit of the risen Christ, we are alive to Christ and called to be his ambassadors (2 Cor 5:17-18). By cooperating with the Spirit's infused faith, hope and love, we are called to bring the transforming power of Christ's new life into our own time and space. Having experienced the healing love of the risen Jesus, living within us and abiding there with his eternal Father through his Spirit of love, we are empowered to take our broken moment in the history of the human race and our place in this disjointed history in order to transform them into something new and wonderful for God.

8. Finally, Paul gives us the authentic measure of how intimately we live in Christ if we allow him and his Spirit to work in our lives. That test of our union with Christ through the trans-

---

[11] Wikenhauser, *op. cit.*, pp. 93-94.

formation of ourselves into living members of the Body of Christ is seen in our loving care and service of others who come into our lives. The love of God that abounds in our hearts through the power of the Spirit (Rm 5:5) must translate into a burning zeal to do God's work and to bring God's creative, healing power to others as "reconcilers" (2 Cor 5:18) of the entire world to God.

Paul wanted to continue his earthly journey of "filling up the sufferings of Christ" in order to become a Jew to the Jews, a Gentile to the Gentiles, weak to the weak, and strong to the strong in order to win them all to Christ. "I do all this for the sake of the good news, so that I too will have a share in it" (1 Cor 9:20-23). Knowing the infinite love of the indwelling Christ for us individually, we wish the whole world to experience such a union in him. The Spirit impels us to go to the lonely and depressed, the anxious and the despondent, to bring them warm, loving hands of comfort and service. To those in sin we wish to be all things to win them to Christ. Caring concern is our way of returning God's love in action as we seek to serve all in need of whatever kind.

Paul never was concerned with describing union with Christ in philosophical, abstract terms. He lived in this loving union with God the Father through Christ and his Spirit. It is for us now to see how this union grows within us through the sacraments, especially the initiation of Baptism and the fullness of encountering Jesus as risen in the Eucharist. It grows through our desire "to pray without ceasing" (1 Th 5:17) as we seek to do the will of God by obeying the Word of God, Jesus Christ, who speaks and guides us through his Spirit. It grows through our discipline to die to all that is within us that is not of Christ and to live lives worthy of Christ as we learn to put on his mind in every event of our lives.

Paul's mystical vision is never a form of Quietism,[12] with-

---

[12] Cf. Leszek Kolakowski, "Quietism" in *The Encyclopedia of Religion* (NY: Macmillan Publishing Co., 1987), Vol. 12, pp. 153-155.

out any thrust outward to build up the Body of Christ. It is an ongoing, active response to return love for love as we live our "new creation" in Christ (2 Cor 5:17). Dying to our own ego-centered, false self, we will see in our oneness with Christ that we are already risen in the Body of Christ. The entire world will look different to us. No longer will we see it solely in the light of the Fall, but in the light of Christ risen, for the world is God's, not the devil's! The resurrection of Jesus becomes the force that spirals the whole universe back into the arms of God from whom it was first born. What happened to Jesus in the resurrection is already happening to us as we rise with him and it will happen to the whole human family and to all creation in the end times.

Christ is the *Alpha* and the *Omega*, at once the center of the material world and its destination, recapitulating the entire cosmos back to the Father. "For in him all the Fullness was pleased to dwell and through him reconciled all things to himself, making peace by the blood of his cross, reconciling everything on earth or in the heavens" (Col 1:20). As we must be changed by many deaths to our false egos and birthed into our true identity, made according to the image and likeness of God (cf. Gn 1:26), that is Jesus Christ, the dark corruption of our ego-mangled world must also dissolve into light.

We do not merely return to our primitive state of Eden at play in the fields of the Lord, but we become the gardeners, unlocking every clod, every lump of matter, that it might grow, bear fruit, nourish the fullness of the "new creation" in Christ. Finally, at the consummate Omega of the material world, wrenched into glory by the birthing hands of God, there will be, as Paul saw, the union of Christ with all of God's material creation coming into its fullness and maturity in Christ so that "Christ is all and in all" (Col 3:11).

4

CHRISTIAN LIVING IN CHRIST

———————— ◊ ————————

As we saw in the preceding chapter describing our union with Christ, the authentic measure of how intimately we live in Christ and allow him and his Spirit to work in our lives, according to Paul, is how lovingly we care for and serve others. In this chapter we wish to examine Paul's writings to see what we must do to intensify our union with the indwelling Christ. The question we pose and seek to answer is: how does the mystical union with the risen Lord Jesus Christ come about?

The Role of Christian Baptism

Paul was constantly preaching to non-baptized adults in order to present his *gospel,* which was for him the revelations he had received directly from the risen Christ and had confirmed by the other apostles of Christ. He was seeking, therefore, to develop in his converts the beginnings of a desire to believe in Jesus Christ, the Son of God, as the way to salvation. Such faith is an acceptance of the *kerygma* or preaching about Christ which cannot be separated from his life, death and resurrection, which constitutes the traditional history of salvation preached and handed down by the early apostles, including Paul.[1] We will develop in a subsequent chapter the qualities of the supernatural aspects of the infused gifts of the Holy Spirit which are given to the convert in Baptism but will require, for our ongoing growth, our diligent cooperation with Christ and the Holy Spirit throughout our entire life. But first let us consider the effects of the sacrament of Baptism.

Baptism according to Paul is the initiation rite which brings about an objective, real union of life with Christ. Being "inserted" into Christ, Christians also enter into the Trinitarian community. This is highlighted in Paul's teaching on Baptism, the initial invitation of the Trinity to share God's very own nature (cf. 2 P 1:4). Baptism institutes an entirely new situation for the newly baptized.

Our incorporation in Christ through Baptism brings about the remission of all our sins:

> Don't you know that those of us who were baptized into Christ Jesus were baptized into his death? Therefore, we were buried with him through our baptism into his death so that just as Christ was raised from the dead by the Father's glory we too might be able to lead a new life.
>
> We know that our old self was crucified with him in order to do away with the sinful self, so we'd no longer be slaves to sin, for a person who has died is set free from sin. But if we've died with Christ we believe that we'll also come to life with him (Rm 6:3-8).

In Gal 3:27, Paul uses the analogy of putting on Christ as putting on a garment that completely covers us. "For all of you who were baptized into Christ have clothed yourselves with Christ." The Greek word, "to baptize," *baptizein*, means to anoint or wash.[2] Its Christian meaning and ritual implies being

---

[1] Cf. Kittel, ed., *op. cit.*, Vol. VI, art., *Pistis,* by R. Bultmann, p. 208.

[2] Cf. Kittel, ed., *op. cit.*, Vol. I, art., *Bapto, Baptizo,* by A. Oepke, pp. 529-546.

plunged into water as a symbol of being completely surrounded by Christ and immersed into his new life.[3]

By such analogies Paul wishes to highlight the complete change that takes place within the Christian by the gratuitous gift of God through Christ and his Spirit. A new life is given to the Christian, which is an ontological reality through the intimate union the Christian shares with the risen Lord Jesus. Such a gift calls Christians to respond to live a new life that excludes sin.[4]

The Coming of the Holy Spirit

Christians in Baptism receive the power of the Holy Spirit so that they can live in Christ and in the Spirit. For Paul one cannot separate the activity of Christ from the activity of the Spirit since they work in *synergy* (together, each person contributing to the achievement of a single over-all effect). The intimate union with Christ is brought about and lived through the working of the Spirit who gives us the power to turn away from the *flesh* and lovingly embrace the will of God (1 Th 5:19; for texts showing the coming of the Spirit in Baptism, cf. 1 Cor 12:13; 6:11; Gal 3:28; 2 Th 2:13).

Justification

Paul, who was trained in the legal terminology of rabbinic law, often used the word *justification* (in Greek, *dikaiosune*)[5] to describe the instantaneous act by which a Christian passes from the state of sin and hostility against God to enter into the

---

[3] Wikenhauser, *op. cit.*, p. 111.

[4] L. Cerfaux, *The Christian in the Theology of St. Paul* (NY: Herder & Herder, 1967), pp. 331-332.

[5] Cf. Kittel, ed., *op. cit.*, Vol. II, art., *Dikaiosune,* by R. Schrenk, pp. 202-210.

state of grace which brings about a filial divinization as children of God. Such justification makes us human beings *just* in
the eyes of God. *Justice* for Paul means that Christians now can
live in perfect harmony and rectitude according to God's will.
Without God's grace this is an impossibility for human beings.
We cannot merit such a gift by our own deeds or good inten-
tions (Gal 2:16; Rm 3:20, 28; 4:1; Eph 2:8).

Faith Is Infused in Baptism

For Paul, faith (in Greek, *pistis*; to believe, *pisteuein*) is a
very rich and complex reality infused into the baptized Christian. It embraces also the infused gifts of the Spirit of hope and
love.[6] Faith adds to the tenets of the Old Testament the message of Jesus Christ, God's only begotten Son, and what the
Triune God has done and will do through him as our Redeemer.
It gives the Christian the power to acknowledge that Jesus is
Lord (1 Cor 12:4), the Son of God from all eternity and the new
Adam. It enables the believer to proclaim the miracle of Christ's
resurrection and his living, active presence in us and in the
Church through the sacraments and the preaching of the Word.

> For if you confess with your mouth that Jesus is Lord and
> believe in your heart that God raised him from the dead,
> you will be saved (Rm 10:9).

To believe in Jesus Christ is the way to salvation. It presupposes an acceptance of the preaching (*kerygma*) about him,
his earthly teachings, his healings and miracles and his free gift
of himself by dying that we might live now in his eternal life.[7]

---

[6] Huby, *op. cit.*, pp. 18-19. Cf. F. Dreyfus, *Maintenant la Foi, L'Esperance et la
Charité Demeurent Toutes Les Trois (1 Cor 13:13)* in *Analecta Biblica, op. cit.*,
Vol. I, pp. 403-412.

[7] Cf. Kittel, ed., *op. cit.*, Vol. VI, art., *Pistis*, by R. Bultmann, pp. 208-228.

In the Old Testament the Jews believed in God on the basis of his acts in human history. In the New Testament Christians believe that God has acted in a special way through his Son. They make, in faith, a radical reorientation toward God whose divine life they share in and through Jesus Christ by the power of the Holy Spirit.

Not only do we believe in Christ, but we respond through his Spirit to obey him as the living Word, active in the Church's preaching as well as in our hearts. John McKenzie writes: "The single act of belief finds its fulfillment in a progressively fuller commitment to Jesus Christ, until it reaches the point where the believer lives with Christ, crucified with him (Gal 2:20)."[8]

Sanctification

The new, divine life of the Trinity given to us in Baptism delivers us from sin and death. Baptism restores to us many of the privileges of the original state of Adam before he had sinned.[9] Paul usually speaks of this as the *new creation* (2 Cor 5:17) of anyone who by Baptism lives in Christ, but he always links this new life with the creation of the first man, since Christ risen is the "second Adam." Yet Paul does so only with his glance directed toward the future, the new messianic age brought about by Christ, the risen Lord (1 Cor 10:11).

Lucien Cerfaux points out for us the importance of the antithesis Paul draws between the first Adam and Christ, especially in Romans 5. We tend to think that redemption is universal because sin had affected all men. "But for Paul, the new life of participation in Christ's life, is prior in God's intention. Since the life of Christ was to affect the whole of the human

---

[8] J. McKenzie, *Dictionary of the Bible* (NY: Bruce Publishing Co., 1965), p. 269.

[9] Jean Danielou, *"Le Symbolisme des Rites baptismaux"* in *Dieu Vivant*, no. 1 (Paris, 1945), p. 1 ff. Cf. M. Barnouin, "Le Caractére Baptismal et Les Enseignements de St. Paul" in *Analecta Biblica*, Vol. II, pp. 299 ff.

race, the divine plan made it necessary that one man should likewise be the initiator of the state of sin, and that sin should spread to all men because of him. Thus, in God's mind, there is a perfect balance between the fall of man and his salvation. Adam is then the 'type' of Christ (Rm 5:14) and the fall is modelled on salvation."[10]

Paul thus shows us that, although because of Adam's sin which has had repercussion on all human beings, yet "the gift is not like the transgression" (Rm 5:15). There is no condemnation now because Christ has offset the sin of Adam which we have all inherited. In God's eternal plan God has decreed that all of us have been created according to the image and likeness of Christ (Gn 1:26-27). He is the Redeemer of all who accept his sanctifying Spirit who brings about, through Christ, our justification and a sharing in divine life, God's grace living in us.

The Christian Life of Tension

The fundamental question that faces us is whether we can live consistently in an intimate union with Christ for ever or whether our life in him, at least on this earth, will be a constant struggle. Paul always sees the Christian life as one of growth in Christ and his Spirit. We must keep in mind and guide our lives according to the basic principles of revealed truth that Christ has given to us through his disciples. To live in Christ is for Paul a reality that frees us from slavery to sin and evil powers (cf. Gal 4; Rm 6). This is because we have the Holy Spirit whose power in us can do more than any evil forces (Rm 8; Eph 1).

But our relationship with Christ can never be achieved solely from God's side. There is no sudden once-and-for-all

---

[10] Cerfaux, *The Christian...*, p. 231.

sanctification. No principalities or demons can ever separate us from Christ. Yet we must stand vigilantly attentive and bring every thought and imagination under control in obedience to Jesus Christ (2 Cor 10:5). We are to watch carefully how we live and not be foolish persons but wise (Eph 5:15-17).

Our sinful nature and ingrained evil habits do not disappear in Baptism, but are with us always and threaten us at all times (Gal 5:16-20). We are able to sin even though Christ has justified us. Paul saw his converts in Corinth and Galatia, for example, turning to sin and creating divisions among themselves even after they had accepted the faith, and it saddened him a great deal.[11] Grace through the Trinitarian indwelling gives us strength, but we must be diligent to die to the "old man" in us and live in obedience to Christ in us (Col 3:8-10).[12]

We are to strive continually as a runner in the stadium to reach our goal, life on high in Christ Jesus. Like St. Paul, we must be able to say: "I forget what's behind me and reach out for what's in front of me. I strain toward the goal to win the prize — of God's heavenward call in Christ Jesus" (Ph 3:13-14).

Spiritual Combat

Paul was extremely disciplined in his spiritual life and fought with God's grace to be delivered from his "unspiritual self" that tempted him to do the things he knew in his "spiritual self" he should not do (Rm 7:16). In his struggle he discovered that in him, as in all human beings, there remained after Baptism a remnant of the "old man" which he referred to

---

[11] Cf. David Wenham, "The Christian Life: A Life of Tension?" in *Pauline Studies*, ed. D.A. Hagner & Murray J. Harris (Grand Rapids, MI: Eerdmans Publ. Co., 1980), pp. 80-94.

[12] C. Boyer, *"Kaine Ktisis" (2 Cor 5:17; Gal 6: 15)* in *Analecta Biblica*, Vol. I, pp. 487-492.

as "sin that dwells in my members" (Rm 7:23). Yet he knew that he could be delivered from this state by cooperating with the grace made available to him "through Jesus Christ our Lord" (Rm 7:25).

We modern Christians are familiar with the meaning of *asceticism*. It comes from the Greek word, *askein* which means to practice or to exercise. In Attic Greek it refers to the exercise of the body or to the practice of an art. It is strange that this word is used only once in the entire New Testament. Paul uses it to indicate how he strove mightily to keep his conscience clear before God and man (Ac 24:16). We find his teaching in this area very down-to-earth as he uses other words to describe the spiritual combat that Christians must enter into against the carnal forces within us that would attack and seek to destroy God's divine life within us.[13]

And he offers us clear instructions on the need for training in bodily and spiritual self-discipline and renunciation in 1 Cor 9:25-27:

> Everyone who competes in an athletic contest trains rigorously, but while *they* do it to win a perishable crown, *we're* competing for an imperishable one. So I don't run as if I didn't know where the finish line is; when I box I don't just punch wildly. On the contrary, I discipline myself and bring my body under control, because I don't want to preach to others and then find myself disqualified.

Mortification

The Greek word, *nekrosis*, death, and the verb, *nekroo*, to put to death, is used by Paul literally in Romans 4:19 to refer to Abraham who did not weaken in faith but considered his

---

[13] Cf. Kittel, ed., *op. cit.*, Vol. I, art., *Askeo,* by L. Windisch, pp. 494-496.

body as already dead. Paul exhorts the Romans "to think of yourselves as being dead to sin and living for God in Christ Jesus" (Rm 6:11). He teaches those who have lapsed from their former state of justification to "put to death those parts of you that are earthly: fornication, impurity, passion, evil desires, and that greed which is idolatry" (Col 3:5).[14]

In Paul's teachings on the necessary discipline needed on our part to cooperate with the indwelling risen Christ, we see his emphasis on the negative side, namely, of removing and avoiding all that might hinder our striving toward greater sanctity in greater union with Christ. But he also emphasizes the positive aspects of such external and internal discipline and encourages us to cooperate with God's grace and to practice the Christian virtues of love and self-sacrifice so as to come into a greater union with God and neighbor. We will develop this more in detail when we deal with the workings of the Holy Spirit in us.

Growth in Christian Freedom

Paul preached unceasingly that by the Spirit of the risen Lord who dwells within us we are set free from any slavery to external forces by an inner revolution as we put on the mind of Jesus Christ and no longer live according to the illusions of the pagans (Eph 4:17). It is the Spirit of God who helps us to die to the "flesh" and live in the spirit. "But you are not in the flesh; on the contrary, you are in the Spirit, since the Spirit of God dwells within you. Anyone who does not have Christ's Spirit does not belong to Christ" (Rm 8:9).

---

[14] Kittel, ed., *op. cit.*, Vol. IV, art., *Nekrosis, Nekroo,* by R. Bultmann, pp. 892-895.

The Infused Gift of Hope

Paul builds his spiritual teaching on the foundation of the infused gifts of the Holy Spirit of faith, hope and love. "So these three — faith, hope and love remain, but the greatest of these is love" (1 Cor 13:13; also, 1 Th 1:3).

We have seen how faith is the Spirit's gift whereby we open up to God's love as especially revealed in Jesus Christ and his loving presence in other human beings. The Spirit grounds us in the foundation of God's infinite love that has elected us to become true children of the Trinitarian community in an ongoing process throughout our entire earthly life. Faith leads us in our spiritual growth to the infused gift of hope (*elpis*). Hope grounds us on God's fidelity to his promise to "justify us" (Rm 8:30).

François Amiot describes the role of hope in the life of the Christian: "We journey by faith and not with clear vision (1 Cor 13:12; 2 Cor 5:7). We bear the seal of the Spirit with a view to the day of redemption (Eph 4:30), and this gift of the Spirit places in our hearts a hope which cannot delude us and which is not in any way weakened but is, rather, strengthened by the tribulations endured for the sake of the gospel (Rm 5:3-5)."[15]

In all our striving to live according to the mind of Jesus Christ, hope contains three elements of (1) the expectation of the "not yet" possessed, (2) trust in God's fidelity and (3) our patient waiting for the fullness of God's promises.[16] For Paul hope is not easily attained but we must struggle to exercise it throughout all our patiently endured sufferings (Rm 5:4). We draw our strength to hope in God as our rock and fortress and find encouragement through Holy Scripture (Rm 15:4).

Hope is most frequently used by Paul to describe our stretching out to attain the fullness of the glorious life to come

---

[15] François Amiot, *The Key Concepts of St. Paul* (NY: Herder & Herder, 1962), p. 234.
[16] Cf. Kittel, ed., *op. cit.*, Vol. II, art., *Elpis,* by R. Bultmann, p. 531.

(Col 1:27) which is already ours in effect when we live in the indwelling presence of the risen Lord (Rm 6:5-11). We Christians have one and the same hope for we are one body in one spirit (Eph 4:4).

Agape

In his First Letter to the Corinthians, Paul has penned one of the most lyrical passages in all of Scripture to describe the importance of the Christian concept of *love*. Here he summarizes the centrality of love of God and neighbor in his use of *agape* and the verb, *agapan*, to refer to the love of God and Christ for all human beings as well as the love we should have for God and Jesus the Lord along with the love we should have mutually for all who are made according to the image and likeness of God.

After exalting love above all other charismatic gifts, he describes true Christian love:

> Love is patient, love is kind. It isn't jealous, doesn't boast, isn't arrogant. Love is not dishonorable, isn't selfish, isn't irritable, doesn't keep a record of past wrongs. Love doesn't rejoice at injustice but rejoices in the truth. Love endures all things, love has complete faith and steadfast hope, love bears with everything. Love never ends.... So these three — faith, hope, and love — remain, but the greatest of them all is love (1 Cor 13:4-13).

In his description of Christian love we see how Paul saw the absolute centrality of love, the "queen of all virtues." Without true love, the infused gift of the Holy Spirit, that abounds in our hearts (Rm 5:5), no virtue or effort would have meaning. Faith and hope, according to Paul, share with love the privilege of having God for the direct object, but will disappear in the glorious life to come, when the justified and holy ones will no longer see darkly as in a mirror (1 Cor 13:12) but will see as they are seen, face to face. And hope will be no more when the possibility of possessing eternal life is a reality.[17]

Love for Paul is the fulfillment of the two great commandments to love God with our whole heart and love our neighbor as we love ourselves (Mt 22:40; Rm 13:9-10). Love is what directs the entire Christian life of perfection and is the goal of all our striving.

The simple goal of all Christians is to progress in prayer and ultimately in our deepest consciousness through faith, hope and especially love that Jesus Christ is totally one with us, imaging the love of the Father through the gift of love, the Holy Spirit (Col 3:14). We are to surrender in each moment our whole being to be directed in every thought, word and deed by the Spirit's loving power.

God Is Love

Love is always an involving caring, a fiery movement toward immanent union through self-emptying devotion. Love, in order to exist in us or in God, must always be pouring itself out from its own abundance, always giving of itself. Tied to the mysterious makeup of God as an *I* that is also a *We* is God's bursting forth from within his own perfect, circular, loving self-containment to embrace us so that we might be transformed by the divinizing power of the Holy Spirit to love all others.

How much of God's fire of love we have allowed to touch ourselves is measured by how much ardent love in service we show to others. We meet God intimately in his total availability, mutual love and self-emptying sacrifice for us in Jesus, God-Man. We are also transformed by the Spirit's gift of love to form

---

[17] The question of these three theological virtues of faith, hope and love in 1 Cor 13:13 remaining forever or only love has been disputed over the ages. Cf. M.F. Lacan, *"Les trois qui demeurent"* in *Recherches de science religieuse* (Paris, 1958), pp. 325 ff., Vol. 46. Also, F. Dreyfus, *op. cit.*

one body with Christ (1 Cor 12:12) as his living members who extend Christ's loving Spirit into the world around us. We are called to live in Christ as a "new creation" (2 Cor 5:17) to minister Christ's reconciliation to a divided world, bringing it back to the Father. "That makes us ambassadors for Christ, just as if God himself were making his appeal through us" (2 Cor 5:20).

Yet how we do this will depend greatly on our talents and state of life. But openness to the world community is a good place to begin. We are called by God to be his cooperators in releasing the inner core of God's love at the heart of all matter.

The more we can act with full consciousness and reflection, the more we humanize ourselves, and the more we also unleash the spiritual powers that enable us to transcend the material, the limited, the particular, and pass over to the realm of enduring and limitless spirit. Paul sees the work of the Holy Spirit necessarily tied to the reconciliation of the entire cosmos back to the heavenly Father in and through Christ, the risen Lord.

Without the Holy Spirit there is no awareness on our part of God's flaming love for us. And there is no true transformation of ourselves into living members of the Body of Christ unless we come to the aid of others in their many needs: "The Spirit we have received is not the spirit of this world but the Spirit that comes from God and enables us to know what it is that God has freely bestowed upon us. And we proclaim this in words taught by the Spirit rather than by human wisdom, words which explain spiritual matters to those who have the Spirit" (1 Cor 2:12-13). It is fitting now to see how Paul develops his teaching on the Holy Spirit in his mystical vision of God in the history of salvation.

5

THE HOLY SPIRIT, GIFT OF GOD'S LOVE

◊

ONE OF PAUL'S ORIGINAL theological contributions to the early Church was his teaching of the dynamic growth of the individual Christian, the Church, and the entire cosmos "in Christ" and "in the Spirit." There is for Paul a connection between the Spirit and the risen Jesus which is not something merely external, but internal and flowing out of their similar activities and natures. Thus for Paul to call us to live and walk in the Spirit (Gal 5:25) is to call us also to live "in Christ" (2 Cor 5:17). These two terms in a special way are nearly interchangeable.[1]

Yet Paul never makes the persons of the Holy Spirit and the Son of God, Jesus Christ, identical. He always uses the phrase, *in Christ*, whenever he is speaking of the preexisting Word of God before the incarnation as well as speaking of Christ's unique role in redeeming us. He usually uses the phrase, *in the Spirit*, to describe the style of life the faithful are to live under the power and wisdom of the Holy Spirit.

Paul often reminds his Christian converts to walk in the

---

[1] On the near equivalency of these two phrases, "in the Spirit" and "in Christ," cf. F. Prat, *The Theology of St. Paul*, Vol. II, tr. by John L. Stoddard (Westminster, MD: The Newman Bookshop, 1958), pp. 292-293; L. Cerfaux, *Christ in the Theology of St. Paul*, *op. cit.*, pp. 284-323; A. Wikenhauser, *op. cit.*, pp. 53-59.

Spirit and not in the flesh by acting in a manner worthy of God (Col 1:10; 1 Th 2:12). Paul refers to the Holy Spirit as being the source of divine power, sent by God through the merits of Christ and his intercession, to effect the work of sanctification or *Christification* of the faithful.[2] In Rm 15:18-19 he clearly distinguishes between the work of Christ and that of the Holy Spirit:

> I don't dare speak of anything except what Christ has done through me to win the obedience of the Gentiles by word and deed, by the power of signs and wonders, and by the power of the Holy Spirit.... As a result, all the way around from Jerusalem to Illyricum, I've completed the proclamation of God's good news.

The Distinction of the Persons of Christ and the Holy Spirit

The Holy Spirit and Christ the Son of God are two distinct persons, both within the Trinity and in their relationships to us in the history of salvation in the Body of Christ, the Church. The preexisting Son of God is never identified with the Holy Spirit in Paul, nor is the historical God-Man the same person as the Holy Spirit. And yet their roles seem to converge when it comes to the sanctification of souls as Prat clearly indicates:

> The points of contact between Christ and the Spirit concern only the glorified Christ, and even this is not in his physical, personal life at the right hand of the Father, but in his mystical life in the bosom of the Church. In other terms, the Holy Spirit and the glorified Christ, who appear everywhere else as two distinct Persons, seem to become identical in their role of sanctifiers of souls (Col 1:19).[3]

---

[2] F. Prat, *op.cit.*, pp. 292-293.
[3] *Ibid.*, pp. 292-293.

Jesus possessed the fullness of the Spirit (Col 2:9). But it was only after his resurrection that he became for us and for himself a "life-giving spirit" (1 Cor 14:45). He is totally "spiritualized" in his new risen life. He is thus, as risen, able to pour out his Spirit upon us in all the Spirit's gifts so that we can live by the Son and also by the Spirit. We are adopted children of the heavenly Father by the Spirit sent by the Son. God the Father adopts us as his children by giving us his Spirit and Christ adopts us also by giving us his Spirit. "If anyone does not have Christ's Spirit, he doesn't belong to Christ" (Rm 8:9).

The Flesh and the Spirit

Paul uses the word *spirit* 146 times in his writings, 117 in his early epistles. One of his key themes is the antithesis between the *flesh* and the *spirit*. *Flesh* (in Greek, *sarx*) represents, for Paul, ourselves in all our creaturehood, not only in our mortality and weakness, but also in our utter estrangement from God through sin. Godliness is represented by the spirit.

This antithesis between the two is developed mainly in Paul's Letter to the Romans, ch. 7 and 8; 1 Corinthians, ch. 2 and 3; and Galatians, ch. 3 and 5. This is not merely a contrast between the inner, spiritual side of us and the outward, physical parts of our existence.[4] "To live according to the spirit" means for Paul that a Christian is to be guided by the Holy Spirit on all levels: body, soul and spirit. This is to be attuned to God's holy will in every thought, word and deed. It is to be a "new creation in Christ" (2 Cor 5:17).

---

[4] Cf. C. Moule, *The Holy Spirit* (Grand Rapids, MI: Wm. B. Eerdmans Publishing Co., 1978), pp. 40-42; Alasdair I.C. Heron, *The Holy Spirit* (Philadelphia: Westminster Press, 1983), p. 39; G.A. Maloney, SJ, *The Cosmic Christ: From Paul to Teilhard* (NY: Sheed & Ward, 1968), p. 21 ff.; G. Montague, SM, *The Holy Spirit: Growth of a Biblical Tradition* (NY: Paulist Press, 1976), p. 39; Kittel, ed., *op. cit.*, Vol. VI, art., *Pneuma,* by E. Schweizer, pp. 396-452.

To the Holy Spirit, Paul assigns the character, initiative, and salvific action proper to a Divine Person who proceeds as the gift of love from the Father and the Son. Paul had discovered, through a personal experience, the world of the Holy Spirit. This for Paul is a "new sphere of life" (Rm 6:4) with the Holy Spirit as the agent that creates this new life. He insisted that we Christians have become alive by the Spirit so we must also then walk by the Holy Spirit (Gal 5:16, 26).

Christians are to be *pneumatikoi*, spiritualized by the Spirit, because the primary function of the Spirit is recognized in the creation of this life in Christ. The possession of the Spirit is not the totality or the fullness of Christian perfection, but the Spirit is given as the "firstfruits" (Rm 8:23) and the pledge or guarantee of its completion (2 Cor 1:22; Eph 1:14). Here we see how the phrases *in the Spirit* and *in Christ* complement one another. The Spirit is given in embryonic form in Baptism to bring about the fullness of Christ's life in us by conforming us gradually through progressive growth to a greater likeness to the image of Christ. "But you are not in the flesh; you are in the spirit, since the Spirit of God dwells in you" (Rm 8:9).

The Father Gives Himself to Us Through His Spirit

The Father promised in the Old Testament to gift us, his chosen people, with his Spirit of love, through whom we can be transformed into new people, with "new hearts," able to keep God's commandments to love him with our whole heart (Dt 6:6) and to love our neighbor as ourselves (Lv 19:18).

Jesus pledges his infallible word over and over in the New Testament that his Father will truly give us his Spirit. The Spirit images the Father's love for his children, and divinizes us, making us his daughters and sons. When we receive this Spirit as gift from the Father by faith (Gal 3:2, 14; Ac 11:17) and in Baptism (1 Cor 6:11; Tt 3:5), the Spirit dwells with us (Rm 8:9; 1

Cor 3:16; 2 Tm 1:14), in our spirit (Rm 8:16; Rm 1:9) and even in our body (1 Cor 6:19).

Christ Also Sends Us His Spirit

The Spirit of the Father is also the gift of the Son (Rm 8:9; Ph 1:19; Gal 4:6). We are enabled to become truly children of God our Father through Jesus, his only begotten Son (Rm 8:14-16; Gal 4:6 ff.). This Spirit acts so that Christ may live in our hearts through faith (Eph 3:16-19). Jesus is God the Father's gift of love to us (Jn 3:16). Yet it is through the Spirit of love that Jesus in his humanity becomes in his death-resurrection the full, perfect image of the Father. Christ is risen from the dead by the power of the Holy Spirit. Because Jesus has the fullness of God's glory, he can send to us the fullness of the Spirit, who allows us to grow into greater glory through our oneness with the risen Lord Jesus.

To the risen Christ, it has been given to bestow upon us the power and glory of God's Spirit. Jesus could not yet give the fullness of the Spirit until he had died (Jn 7:39 ff.). But now Jesus sends us the fullness of God's gift of love, the Spirit, who convinces us that the risen Lord lives within us (Rm 8:11). By his victory over sin and death, Jesus is able to dwell within us and assure us that the Holy Spirit is the Father's definitive gift of love. The risen Jesus and the Holy Spirit can never be separated, nor can the Father, since the Spirit is their mutual love dwelling within us as their supreme gift to us.

The Spirit Makes Christ Present to Us

The Spirit does not only bring Jesus' risen presence to his disciples, who knew him in his lifetime. He is as well the Father's gift of eternal love to everyone who wishes to call Jesus Lord and Master through the same Spirit (1 Cor 12:4). The Spirit, as the image of Christ, makes it possible for us to enter into an intimate friendship with Jesus that is more powerful, more lasting than any such with him before he died. The Spirit makes Jesus present with all power and love. Through the Spirit we touch the same Jesus who walked this earth. We can hear him teach through the Spirit.

Jesus risen still heals through the Spirit as he did on earth. The Spirit makes it possible for us to continually change our lives. The Holy Spirit gives us his fruit: "The Spirit's fruit is love, joy, peace, patience, kindness, goodness, faith, gentleness, self-control.... If we live by the Spirit, let us follow the Spirit's lead" (Gal 5:22, 25).

The Spirit of Holiness

The gift of God's love, the Spirit, is also called in Scripture *Holy*. As all three Persons of the Trinity are spirit, so all three are holy. Yet the Holy Spirit is in a very special and unique way Holiness itself. All holiness in God is found in God's self-sacrificing love. But if the Spirit is Love, we should be able also to call the Spirit the Holy One.

In Scripture, whenever God is described as holy, he is always close to angels or human beings, involved in communicating his loving nature to others (cf. Lv 11:44-45). God's holiness is seen as he gives himself to us as a gift of love so we can truly participate in his very nature (2 P 1:4). Yet this loving union does not dissolve God and ourselves into one being.

Teilhard de Chardin gives us a pithy, but powerful statement that well describes the work of the Holy Spirit in bringing about our union with the Trinity: "Love differentiates as it unites."[5] It is the Holy Spirit who brings about an ecstatic union

---

[5] Teilhard de Chardin, *The Phenomenon of Man*, tr. Bernard Wall (London: Wm. Collins Sons and Co., 1959), pp. 264-267.

that draws out at the same time the very uniqueness of the *I* and the *Thou* and the *We*. God's unique Love, the *We*, is the work of the Holy Spirit who not only unites us with the Trinitarian community of divine life, but at the same time makes us unique in our personhood as he makes the Father uniquely our Father and the Son uniquely our Savior and brother (Eph 4:4).

God does not primarily give us a mere "thing" or a created grace, but gives us himself as perfect love and perfect holiness. Thus we call God's personification of his self-giving love the Holy Spirit. The Spirit of the risen Lord brings us into the holiness of the Trinity. Dwelling within us in deepest intimacy of total self-emptying love, God becomes present to us as holiness itself in his Spirit of love. Love brings communion, and in this intimate communion with the indwelling Trinity, we are made holy, authentic children of God (Rm 8:15-16).

The Spirit is revealed in the joy of the Savior and his intimacy with the Father, all living intimately within us.

Grace and the Working of the Holy Spirit

The notion of grace (*charis* in Greek) in St. Paul is very complex. It, along with the word *charisma, charismata*, always emphasizes in Paul's writings the free, gratuitous gift or gifts of God to us, his chosen children.[6] In discussing the Law of the Old Testament in the light of the grace of the New Testament in and through Jesus and the Holy Spirit, Paul writes: "... where sin increased grace increased even more, so that just as sin reigned in death so too should grace reign in reconciliation leading to eternal life through our Lord Jesus Christ" (Rm 5:20-21).

---

[6] Cf. Kittel, ed., *op. cit.*, Vol. IX, art., *Charis,* by H. Conzelmann, pp. 387-415.

Created and Uncreated Grace

The perennial problem in Christianity has always been: how does God, if he is perfect and immutable, communicate with us, his human children? Grace, for St. Thomas Aquinas, was a created, static "thing," an "entity" which God would send down upon our human natures to give us the ability to communicate with the Trinity. Thomas saw grace as an "entitative habit,"[7] the originating "principle of meritorious action by the intermediary action of the virtues."[8]

Such an impersonal and static view contradicts Paul's concept of grace which he roots always within the interpersonal relationships of the Trinity toward God's created world, especially toward us human beings. Karl Rahner captures the Pauline concept of grace in this way:

> Each one of the three divine persons communicates himself to us in gratuitous grace in his own personal particularity and diversity. This Trinitarian communication is the ontological ground of our life in grace and eventually of the direct vision of the divine persons in eternity.[9]

The early Eastern Fathers of the Church, more biblically and mystically oriented in the thinking of St. Paul, help us better to understand the Pauline doctrine of grace. They have distinguished God's gratuitous, graceful relationships with us and his created world from God's ineffable and incomprehensible essence or divine nature that is truly immutable and unchanging. We can never totally communicate with God in his essence (Ex 33:23). But the good news Jesus has revealed to us through his Spirit and that Paul continually preached is that the Trinity

---

[7] Thomas Aquinas, *De Veritate*, 27, 2 & 7.

[8] Thomas Aquinas, *Summa Theologica*, I-II, q. 110, a. 4.

[9] K. Rahner, *Nature and Grace*, tr. Dinah Wharton (London: Sheed & Ward, 1963), p. 24.

now abides within us and communicates to us in the most intimate union of love through divine "uncreated energies."

Such a distinction preserves the awesome transcendence of God and his Trinitarian, personalized gifts of Father, Son and Spirit to us. The whole message of the good news consists in God's revelation of himself as a loving Father, giving himself to us through his Son, Jesus Christ, in his Spirit. In that experience we can know God in his love toward us through his energies of love.

These energies can never be conceived of as created "things," but rather as God — Father, Son and Holy Spirit — personally working in all the events of our lives, to give themselves to us in loving union.[10] These uncreated energies are not externalized gifts of God, but God himself, giving himself to us in the free gift of each of the Persons in the Trinity. They are called "uncreated" energies because their origin is the essence of God himself, who cannot be limited by time and space. His love endures forever.

Through these energies, God, as it were, goes beyond himself and becomes "transradiant" in order to communicate himself in a true union of himself with us.

Created Graces

The uncreated energies we can call "primary grace," and Paul saw the Spirit as the agent bringing a share of God's divine life, love and fellowship to us. "The grace of the Lord Jesus Christ, the love of God, and the fellowship of the Holy Spirit be with you all!" (2 Cor 13:13).

Our sanctification or divinization by grace is primarily effected by the indwelling Spirit, but also by the accompanying created grace, which is always, according to Paul, inseparable

---

[10] Cf. my work on this subject, *Uncreated Energy* (Amity, NY: Amity House, 1987).

from the Spirit. It is never a static or impersonal, created entity, totally removed from the primal grace of the Holy Spirit who is "the Spirit of grace" (Heb 10:29). Thus grace according to Paul is always present in interpersonal relationships between the Trinity and ourselves by the working of the Spirit.

Deep in the core of our being the Trinity dwells as tri-personal uncreated energy which is imparted to us as love by the Holy Spirit. As we open ourselves to receive God's love as *grace* or gift, the Spirit brings about a personal, loving relationship between ourselves and the Trinity that we call *sanctifying*. This is a subjective disposition, a vital consciousness on our part that we are holy because the God who dwells within us, purifying our hearts, is holy. We often hear the expression that one is in the state of sanctifying grace. This state provides the context for an affective and effective dialogue between the indwelling Trinity and the individual Christian through the Holy Spirit.

The Dynamism of Grace

Paul saw *grace* primarily as the Trinity's free, gratuitous gift of self to us whom God has called in Christ Jesus "to be holy and blameless before him and to live in his love" (Eph 1:4). God's self-giving love confers upon us a condition that is completely beyond our own power to attain or hold on to. It is God the Father who calls us to an "I-Thou" relationship as his living children. We are inserted into a real, vital and dynamic oneness with Jesus Christ as living members of his Mystical Body, the Church.

But we are called to *respond* to this dynamic, graceful relationship. We need to accept this awesome dignity to which God is calling us at all times, in all circumstances. *Sanctifying grace* according to Paul is seen as the work chiefly of the Holy Spirit, who can never be personally separated from God's love given and our love returned. Thus we can understand how *sanctifying grace* can grow without any limits except those we humanly place on God's uncreated energies of love.

Therefore, with Paul, we must conclude that *sanctifying grace* is not an extrinsic, created quality, outside of this hidden relationship, grounded on the Spirit's gifts of faith, hope and love. Fr. Luis Bermejo grasps well St. Paul's understanding of created grace in the context of our interpersonal relationship with the Trinity:

> Sanctifying grace is rather a new subjective disposition, a new attitude with regard to God that can best be described as an intimately personal relationship with him, an essential element in the affective and effective dialogue between the indwelling God and the believer who is indwelt.[11]

Spirit Discernment

One of the important gifts of the Spirit in Paul's list of charisms (*charismata*) given in 1 Cor 12:8 ff. is that of *discernment*. Are we being guided by the Holy Spirit or by some other false spirit in our relationships with God and other persons? This Paul calls in Greek, *diakrisis*, a judgment, guided by the Spirit, that allows us to see correctly from God's point of view what would be in accord with God's will and glory. Guidelines in the New Testament are found in Mt 7:15-23; 1 Cor 12:3; 1 Jn 4:1-6. This gift is a special knowledge given by the Spirit to build up the community of the Church through the greatest gift of the Spirit: love.

In Paul's beautiful paean to true love, he gives us the ultimate discernment of Spirit-guided activities: Without true love,

---

[11] Luis Bermejo, SJ, *The Spirit of Life* (Chicago: Loyola University Press, 1989), p. 169.

all other seeming gifts of the Spirit are nothing. Love alone will last forever (cf. 1 Cor 13 ff.).

Praying in the Spirit

When we do not know how to pray as we ought, the Holy Spirit comes to help us in our weakness. The Spirit himself expresses our plea in a way that could never be put into words (Rm 8:26-27). This means more than singing in tongues. It is a nonverbal type of prayer that comes from the core of our being where the Spirit dwells and infuses his gifts of faith, hope and love.

Paul taught all his converts to live always in the presence of God dwelling as Trinity within them. "Rejoice always. Pray without ceasing" (1 Th 5:16-17). This is what God expects of us in Christ Jesus. The Spirit gives us an inner perception of our dignity as children of God. This gives us a Spirit-filled freedom (2 Cor 3:17-18) to dispose of our lives in every moment according to the good pleasure of the heavenly Father. It is through the infused gifts of faith, hope and love, exercised by us in each living situation that we live true, Christian lives.

The Charismata of the Holy Spirit

Besides sanctifying grace, the Holy Spirit helps us through his special gifts, fruits and virtues (theological and moral) to make us holy and blameless children of God and living members of Christ's Body. We should not separate in our experience, as the saints and mystics never did, the grace of the virtues and that of the gifts of the Spirit.

The Spirit of love invades all our faculties and covers all our actions, so that, as we cooperate with God's graces, we can develop the supernatural habits or virtues needed to live an integrated and holy life unto the glory of God. Love of God must permeate all the details of our human life and conduct. The Spirit is the fundamental gift in his person as he adapts himself to our situations and circumstances. The Spirit develops love in us in many ways, forms and manifestations.

As Yves Congar points out,[12] the scriptural source of the theology of the gifts of the Spirit is the messianic text of Isaiah 11:1-2:

> The Spirit of the Lord shall rest upon him,
> a spirit of wisdom and understanding,
> a spirit of counsel and of strength,
> a spirit of knowledge and of fear of the Lord.

The Septuagint Greek version of the Old Testament adds to fear the virtue of piety, thus giving us the traditional seven gifts of the Holy Spirit. The Spirit helps us through these gifts to effect the work of our sanctification. The Spirit works through our developed virtues that are permeated by the Spirit's grace, but the gifts are the operations of the Spirit operating freely, immediately, and directly upon us.

The Spirit: The Soul of the Mystical Body

Thus we see that the Holy Spirit is both the gift of love and in this supreme gift, the Spirit is the giver of sanctifying and actual graces of innumerable descriptions:

> There are various gifts, but the same Spirit, there are various ministries, but the same Lord, and there are various ways to be active, but the same God who causes all these effects in everyone. Some manifestation of the Spirit is given to each for the common good (1 Cor 12:4-7).

---

[12] Yves Congar, OP, *I Believe in the Holy Spirit*, tr. David Smith (NY: Seabury Press, 1983), Vol. 2, p. 134.

Jesus lives in us through the charisms that his Spirit effects for the good of the whole. Our God-given talents become true charisms under the development of the Spirit when we cover them with the Spirit's graces and use them to build up the Body of Christ, the Church. "Grace has been given to each of us according to the extent of Christ's gift" (Eph 4:7). The list Paul gives in 1 Cor 12:8-10 was not meant by him to be an exclusive list but rather enumerates the nine gifts of the Spirit that Paul saw as necessary in building up the "charismatic" prayer community of Corinth. These are: wisdom, knowledge, faith, healing, miracles, prophecy, discernment, speaking in tongues and interpretations of the tongues. "One and the same Spirit produces all of these, distributing them individually to each person as he wishes" (1 Cor 12:11).

Another list of special charisms can be found in the social and teaching gifts given by Christ for the building up of the Church:

> You are the body of Christ, and each individual is a member. God has appointed some in the church to be, first, apostles, second, prophets, third, teachers, then miracle workers, those with the gift of healing, helpers, administrators, and those with various tongues.... But strive for the greatest gifts (1 Cor 12:27-31).

The Holy Spirit and Resurrection

We will see in the next chapter how the Spirit builds up the Body of Christ, the Church. We still need, however, to highlight the role of the Holy Spirit in manifesting the presence of the risen Lord Jesus, both in the individual Christian as well as in the Church and in the eschatological completion of all things in Christ risen.

The work of the risen Christ is to release the Spirit so that we may share abundantly, even now, in his resurrectional life.

The presence of the Holy Spirit living within us is not a sweetness or consolation to be enjoyed without reference to daily living and growth into greater life as children of God. The indwelling Spirit prods us to enter into the death-resurrection dialectic that Jesus lived as he in his humanity marched to his "hour."

He stimulates us to greater complexity, to greater pruning and inner discipline, all in order that the risen life of Jesus might be shared by us. Paul constantly shows us that we are being caught between two opposing forces operating in our lives at all times: the power of darkness and evil and the power of the Spirit of the risen Jesus. This Spirit creates the new life of Christ within us. He also fosters and brings it to fullness or completion in the proportion that the Spirit becomes normative in guiding us to make choices according to the mind of Christ.

The outpouring of the Spirit by the risen Jesus is the filling up in our hearts of the love of God (Rm 5:5). We are able to love at each moment with the very love of God abiding within us. This Spirit is the same love with which God the Father loves his Son and ourselves in him as his children. We are to yield to this inner power and live in it in all our human relationships.

To Build a Community

The work of the Holy Spirit is to reveal to us, not only that we are God's children united to the risen Savior, but also that we must go out and bring the good news of the victory of the risen Lord to all human beings who are also called to share our oneness in the only begotten risen Lord. Jesus extends his anointed work through his Spirit poured out on his members to take away sins, liberate people from division and separation, and bring about the reconciliation of the entire world to the Father in fulfillment of his eternal plan when he created all things in and through his Word (2 Cor 5:17-19; Col 1:18-20).

The final glory of the Body of Christ risen is being realized even now as we learn to surrender ourselves in loving service to each other through the Spirit of the risen Lord. The resurrection is a process of coming into the glory of the whole Christ. This takes place gradually through the symbol of the cross and death, a symbol of ongoing purification and conversion away from the darkness of egoism to embrace and live in the inner light of Jesus risen and living within us and in his Church. Resurrection is a series of saying "yes" to the dictates of Jesus' Spirit. We have the dignity and the duty, both in this earthly existence and in the life to come to manifest the fullness of Christ's glory by our service within the Body of Christ to extend God's gift of reconciliation to all.

6

THE BODY OF CHRIST: THE CHURCH

◊

W<small>E HAVE SEEN THAT</small> Paul built up a Christian mystical vision around the concept of a mystical communion between the individual believer and Christ, the risen Lord. Now we can work out a detailed Pauline mysticism of the community of Christians living in Christ by developing Paul's gradual vision of his ecclesiology.

"Saul, Saul, why are you persecuting me?" (Ac 9:4). From the first encounter with Jesus Christ, Paul met the Savior of the world as the cosmic Christ present in the members of his Church. He had set out to persecute the followers of the man named Jesus, who had been put to death in Jerusalem for blasphemously claiming, in substance, that he was God. But along the road to Damascus, Saul became Paul, and Jesus became for him the living Son of God, "... the image of the unseen God, the firstborn of all creation. For in him all things in the heavens and on earth were created" (Col 1:15-16).

That haunting voice seared Paul's entire being and would never be forgotten. The implications of Christ's words gradually became clearer to him through years of various prayerful encounters with his Lord. A steady progression in Paul's thought can be discerned in his epistles, as his Christology takes more specific and more extensive form. Many modern New Testament exegetes have pointed out the gradual development of Paul's Christology as he composed his pastoral letters to answer exigencies that arose in the early Christian communities which he administered.

In the initial stage of development, we find the Pauline emphasis placed on a basic creed that was formulated undoubtedly by the first church-community in Jerusalem. The death and resurrection of Jesus Christ were professed in faith by the Church as a pledge of future resurrection and entrance into the heavenly kingdom. Paul stresses our own future resurrection which will be realized when Christ returns triumphantly in his *parousia* (1 and 2 Th and 1 Cor 15).

Paul next develops the concept of the power of Christ's death and resurrection, not as looking forward to the *parousia*, but here and now exerting its influence in the life of the individual Christian. Through his glorious resurrectional life Jesus Christ lives in a new way in the souls of his followers. The paschal mystery of Christ's death and resurrection is played out in the life of each and every Christian even in this life (Rm and 1 Cor). Christians "die" to themselves and are "raised" to a new life, the very life of Christ, by which they are changed from the "old man" to the "new man," always "in Christ."

Encountering among the Corinthians and Galatians the heresies of Gnostic Judaisers, heavily influenced by the pagan "mystery" cults, Paul developed the dimensions of his cosmic Christology. Here he strove to define more precisely Christ's relationship, not only to individual human beings, but also to the whole cosmos. Christ appears as the unifying center of all things, drawing all things back to their origins in God. Since the world was created for Christ and by him (Col 1:6), it must be recapitulated or reestablished in and through him under whose power all creatures must one day be united.

Even though Paul gradually and continually developed his Christology and along with it his ecclesiology, it is in his letters of captivity, especially to the Colossians and Ephesians, that we find the full development of Paul's thought.

An Ecclesial Christology

Absorbed by the thought of this new life in Christ, Paul moved easily between the levels where he found this new life in the process of dynamic, progressive growth, namely, the level of the individual, and that of the Christian community. He gives small attention to distinguishing whose perfection is being built up, the individual Christian's or that of the whole Christian community, the Church. The reason is that he saw these levels, not as distinct areas of activity and life, but as two points of view of the identical reality, the life of the Christ, living in both the individual and in the united members of his Body, the Church.

Further, he knew that no individual sanctity could grow outside of the organism that he fondly called the *Body of Christ.* The Church grew in sanctity as the life of Christ developed in the individual members. To understand more clearly this Pauline ecclesiology, let us look at his conception of Christ's Church as the Body of Christ.

You Are Christ's Body

Paul uses the Greek word, *ekklesia,* about sixty times, and with a variety of meanings. In the Old Testament there were two Hebrew words, *qahal* and *edah,* which referred almost synonymously to the religious assembly of the chosen people of Israel.[1] The Septuagint, the Greek translation of the Old Testament, renders the first term, *qahal,* by the Greek word, *ekklesia,* literally "the called out people, chosen by God." The second term, *edah,* was translated by the Greek word, *synagoge.* Paul and the other early teachers of the Church preferred to distinguish the Body of Christ as the *ekklesia* or the "chosen ones in

---

[1] Prat, *op. cit.,* p. 277.

Christ Jesus" (Eph 1:4) to distinguish the Christian Church from
the place of worship for the Jews still under the Old Law.[2]

Various Pauline Meanings of Church

We see an evolution in Paul's ecclesial thought as found
in his epistles. Most frequently, at least in his earlier letters, he
uses this word to refer to a local church or a concrete assembly of Christian believers, for example, "When you assemble
as a church I hear that there are divisions among you" (1 Cor
11:18). "The churches of Asia greet you" (1 Cor 16:19). In other
places he refers to the universal Church, transcending any local congregational boundaries: "God has appointed some in the
Church to be, first, apostles…" (1 Cor 12:28). And again, "You've
heard what my life was like in Judaism, that I went to extraordinary lengths in persecuting the Church of God and trying to
destroy it" (Gal 1:13).

Thus we see that the Church, whether local or universal,
was conceived as a community (*koinonia*) of believers linked
together by the bonds of faith, by the sacraments, especially
Baptism, which incorporated the members into the community,
and especially by the Eucharist, which not only symbolized the
union of the members with the physical Body of Christ, but
greatly deepened this union. Not less, this community was
bound by its obedience to the bishops and presbyters empowered by Christ to teach his word with his authority.

For Paul the Church is not the sum of all believers nor the
total of all the individual communities or local churches.[3] As
Prat states it: "The Church is neither the aggregate of the believers, nor the sum total of the individual communities, but a
moral being to which unity is essential."[4] Prat quotes from

---

[2] Kittel, ed., *op. cit.*, Vol. III, art., *Ekklesia,* by K.L. Schmidt, pp. 501-536.
[3] *Ibid.*, p. 506.
[4] Prat, p. 279.

Harnack: "Not only is the part in the whole, but the whole is in the part."[5]

The Body of Christ

In stressing the living Christ as the source of the common, supernatural life within the believing Christians, Paul moved only gradually to a greater emphasis on the Church as identified in some manner with the physical, resurrected Body-Person, Jesus Christ. In Paul's major epistles, especially to the Romans and to the Corinthians, the concept of the Church as the Body of Christ was not fully developed:

> For just as we have many members in one body and all the members don't have the same functions, in the same way we, many as we are, are one body in Christ, and each one of us is a part of the other (Rm 12:4-5).

> Just as the body is one but has many members, all the members of the body — many though they are — are one body, and so it is with Christ. We've all been baptized in one Spirit into one body, whether Jew or Greek, slave or free, and we've all drunk of one Spirit.... Now you are the body of Christ and each individual is a member (1 Cor 12:12-27; cf. also: 1 Cor 6:12-20; 1 Cor 10:17).

But in the letters to the Colossians and Ephesians, Paul clearly states that the Church is identified with the Body and Christ is the Head. In these two letters the doctrine of the Christian people as the Body of Christ now occupies a clear and central position. "Christ is head of the church, and is himself the savior of the body" (Eph 5:23). He loves this Body, the Church, nourishing it and cherishing it. Because we are members of his body (cf. Eph 5:30), Christ is

---

[5] *Ibid.*, ftnote 1.

> ... the head, from which the whole body, with its joints and ligaments, receives what it needs and is held together, deriving its growth from God (Col 2:19).

> By speaking the truth in love, we'll grow in every way into him — Christ — who is the head upon whom the whole body depends. Joined together and united by all the supporting ligaments, when each part is working as it should the head causes the body to grow and build itself up in love (Eph 4:16; cf. Col 1:18, 24; Eph 1:22, 23; 4:15; 5:23).

Modern scholars, such as Pierre Benoit, John A.T. Robinson, Lucien Cerfaux, Joseph Huby and Alfred Wikenhauser have insisted strongly on the realism intended by Paul in the use of the term "Body of Christ," as applied to the Church. The Church is intimately related to the resurrected Body-Person, Jesus Christ (Eph 2:20-23).

Various Meanings of the Word "Body"

We are dealing with something more than a mere metaphor. The term "body (*soma*) of Christ," as used in the New Testament and especially by Paul, can refer (1) to the historical body of Christ that the apostles knew so intimately during the public years of his life; (2) to the resurrected and glorious body of Christ, ascended into glory; (3) to his body in the Holy Eucharist; and, finally, (4) to Christ's Church.

There is absolute identity between Christ's earthly historical body and his glorified body that lives today, spiritualized and transcending all space and time. The Body of Christ that the Church is, is not ontologically identical with the historical, now glorified body of Christ. Yet in a very real sense there is a partial identity insofar as the life that infuses its members is identical with the divine life of the physical Christ. Although Christians in Baptism, and more so in the Eucharist, come into contact with the same divine life, they retain their own individual, human personalities and life.[6]

Benoit describes this union as a kind of "physical (sacramental) union of the body of the Christian with the individual body of Christ."[7] It is the spiritual (*pneumatic*) body of the living, risen Christ (1 Cor 15:44) that is the carrier of the regenerated life of salvation to our souls. "Without a doubt," continues Benoit, "this 'physical' reality is of a very special type, completely new which is that of the eschatological era begun — while the old era still continues."[8]

Robinson comments that the term, *Mystical Body*, as understood by Western minds today has the connotation of an ethereal union. Such a connotation lessens the understanding of the physical reality of this union between Christ and the community of believing Christians in the Church. Surely one regrets the false concepts that the word "*mystical*" conjures for us, and we could perhaps desire an expression more apt for modern times to describe the very concrete, physical reality of this unique union with Christ's life.

Yet the expression, *Mystical Body*, has a legitimate theological development that through the centuries has steered a clear course in describing this unique union so as to avoid a purely physical concept on the one hand and a purely moral aggregate on the other. Further, it has received the sanction of papal teaching in the encyclical, *Mystici Corporis Christi*, which contains all the elements that modern exegetes of St. Paul have been trying to elucidate.[9]

Christ, living his glorified, resurrectional life, is, through

---

[6] Kittel, ed., *op. cit.*, Vol. VII, art., *Soma*, by E. Schweizer, pp. 1080-1081.

[7] Pierre Benoit, *"Corps, tête et plerome dans le Epitres de la Captivité"* in *Exegese et Theologie* (Paris, 1961), p. 147.

[8] *Ibid.*

[9] Karl Rahner, *L'Appartenance a l'Eglise d'apres la Doctrine de l'Encyclique, "Mystici Corporis Christi"* in *Ecrits Theologiques II* (Bruges, Desclée, 1959), pp. 97-112.

his physical, bodied Person, still the causal means of contact and union with the members of his Church. He gives to them his risen life so that they, with him, forming the Church, are truly forming the *Mystical Body* of Christ. In order to see the points of identity and the points of difference, we must see how the body, the Church, can grow with Christ as its head.

Christ, The Head of the Body-Church

In 1 Cor 12:12-27, cited above, the head is included as a member of the whole body with no conscious reference on Paul's part to Christ. Yet the idea of the head viewed as the director of the whole body is implied by Paul. In the captivity letters, Paul gradually reaches the final development of his teaching by designating Christ as head of his body, the Church. In Col 2:10 Christ is pictured as head of all the principalities and powers, in the sense of superior, or sovereign, having complete authority over them and all other created orders of beings. But in Ephesians, we find Paul's fullest development of this theme:

> He has put all things under his feet and has given him as head over all things to the Church, which is his body, the fullness of the One who fills all things in their totality (Eph 1:22-23).

Christ is the head of the Church, as having supreme authority over its members. Yet Paul's is a deeper insight: the head of a physical body is conceived also as the principle of life, the mover, the nourisher and sustainer of life. "In Christ the fullness of divinity dwells in bodily form and in him you reach completion; he is the head of every ruler and power" (Col 2:10). "By speaking the truth in love we'll grow in every way into him — Christ — who is the head upon whom the whole body depends. Joined together and united by all the supporting ligaments, when each part is working as it should, the head causes the body to grow and build itself up in love" (Eph 4:16). This intuition of Christ as head, as the source of life and activity, is here only hinted at. We shall see now how Paul expresses it even more explicitly.

Building Up the Body of Christ

Paul's clearest statement that Christ is the head of his body, the Church, and of how it grows, is found in Ephesians 4:10-16. Christ is pictured as filling the entire universe from the highest to the lowest reaches of the heavens and earth that he might "fill all things" (Eph 4:10). We have seen that Christ's body, the Church, is "the fullness of the One who fills all things in their totality" (Eph 1:23). In Greek Paul uses present participle, *pleroumenou*, i.e., "the one who fills" all the members with all graces. This is continually going on within the individual members of the Church. Through them Christ is being extended to the world to fill it also with his saving power.

This is why Paul can immediately pass to a brief description of the hierarchical divisions in the Church (Eph 4:11-13), all for the same purpose of "building up the body of Christ, until we all attain to unity of faith and knowledge of the Son of God." Paul says that Christ gives his gifts to the hierarchy "…to equip the saints for the work of ministry, the building up of the body of Christ" (Eph 4:12). The Greek verb, *katartizo*, means "to restore to a complete or correct condition." It implies, also, bringing a being to a perfection which it has never attained before, but one that is in keeping with its given nature and its potentialities.

Thus we could paraphrase this Pauline thought: the purpose of Christ's filling all the universe with his gifts is to perfect the saints (the Christians in whom Christ lives) in order that they may be able to accomplish the great work of service to be rendered in the Church, so that by their works they may build up the total body of Christ. The hierarchical officials, appointed by Christ, are to organize the members for service in the Church. Every Christian has some gift or gifts to develop and contribute to the building up of the Mystical Body of Christ. Church officials have the task of establishing the most favorable conditions so that each member may be stimulated to live fully according to those gifts given to each one.

Human Cooperation to Build Up the Church

Over and over in his epistles Paul emphasizes the importance of the activities of each individual member in building up the Church by his or her responsible cooperation with God's gifts. He does not employ a concept of natural growth, that is, growth that would result without much reflective cooperation on the part of the growing body. Here and now Christians are building up the Church (*oikodome*, the word Paul uses, means "to build a house") by their conscious activities, in cooperation with its head from whom flow the gifts of grace.

The building up of the Church has as its goal to "attain to unity of faith and knowledge of the Son of God — to mature manhood, to the extent of Christ's full stature" (Eph 4:13). Therefore, each member's activity is a vital part of a whole process that is progressing toward a goal which will assuredly be reached one day. The Mystical Body of Christ has, in embryonic form from its very beginning, the fullness that God destined for it. But only through the individual efforts of each member inserted as vibrant parts of a living whole can this fullness be attained.

Christians are immature if they do not let the full life of Christ "apprehend" or "seize" them. They will remain "infants," swayed by false teachings and social values (Eph 4:14; 1 Cor 1:3). Christians mature by acquiring a deeper faith and knowledge of Christ. The sign of their maturity will be measured by their degree of unity in their faith and knowledge of the Son of God and by the extent to which they have put on the "new man" (Eph 2:5; 4:24), Jesus Christ. They are to put aside the selfish egoism of children to grow into the fullness of Christ, the perfect man.

Pope Pius XII phrased it thus in his encyclical, *Mystici Corporis Christi*: "The mystical head, which is Christ, and the Church... constitute one new man. We call Christ the head, and the body, the whole Christ." Our individual perfection is linked to but not limited by the perfection of the body, the Church, and is measured according to the degree of our conscious union with Christ, our head.

The means of growing into greater unity and stability in Christ are expressed in Paul's words, "by speaking the truth in love, we'll grow in every way into him — Christ — who is the head" (Eph 4:15). This would mean living an authentic Christian life in a *divine milieu* where we are progressively more and more aware of being surrounded by the Triune God's uncreated energies of love in every situation. Faith, as Paul says in 2 Th 2:12, accepts the truth, but the truth is lived in love. Love makes the truth manifest. We live by the truth only when we are impelled to do so by love for God and neighbor. "And the truth will set you free" (Jn 8:32).

Our entire Christian life, therefore, must be guided by this single aim: to live the truth in love. This means to do at every moment God's will as discovered in a conscience informed by grace, guiding the total person to act only and always out of love for God and neighbor. But such a union in the Body of Christ cannot be achieved, nor can we act out of love for God, except through Christ, the source of all true, spiritual growth.

Growth in Christ

All growth is from Christ, our head, and we his members who live through and with him. The head gives us members of his body growth only where there is a conscious effort on the individual's part to make a living contact with Christ, the source of all grace. Paul uses many images and symbols to highlight our individual and collective union with Christ and our duty within that collectivity to live the truth in love. The best known image to express the unity between Christ the head and his living members is Paul's use of the allegory of the human body. Our human bodies possess several members: a head, eyes, ears, hands, feet, etc. No such bodily members can function outside of a unity within the entire body. Not one individual member can boast that it is superior to the other members or that it does not need any other members or that it is the entire body. All members are necessary and must be honored and respected.

To show this important principle regarding the members of the Church in relationship to Christ, their head, and to the other members, Paul writes:

> But God has formed the body in such a way as to give greater honor to the members which lack it, so that there will be no discord in the body and the members will feel the same concern for one another. If one member suffers, all the members suffer; if one member is honored all the members rejoice. You are the body of Christ, and each individual is a member (1 Cor 12:24-27).

The Church: Christ's Bride

Paul presents us with another metaphor, that of spouses. He points out that roles of dominance and submission must always be lived out in love, and adds the concept that this intimate union results in new life, divine life, brought about solely by Christ the Spouse. Christ is the source of this divine life, not only for his bride, the Church, but also, through his activity in the Church, for the individual members:

> The man who loves his wife loves himself, for no one ever hates his own flesh. On the contrary, he nourishes and cares for it just as Christ does for the Church, because we are members of his body (Eph 5:28-30).

Paul seizes upon the analogy of a building to convey in another manner the intimate union of Christ with the individual members in whom he lives by his own divine life:

> So then you're no longer strangers and aliens but fellow citizens with the saints and members of God's household. You were built upon a foundation of apostles and prophets, and Christ Jesus was its cornerstone. In him the whole building is joined together and grows into a holy temple in the Lord, and in him you are being built together into God's dwelling place in the Spirit (Eph 2:19-22).

Without Christ there would be no foundation for this life in the Spirit. It is clear that Paul does not signify a moral entity by the term, Christ, that would include both Christ personally and the body of the faithful united with him. Christ is always the historical individual, now sharing through his resurrection and the outpouring of the Spirit his divine life with us as we are intimately connected to him by our living the truth in love.

Love proven by actions is the propulsion that moves a Christian toward Christ. But the more a single member loves Christ through the love of his or her neighbor, the more the whole body becomes "full" of the love of Christ, loving his body, which is the Church.

The One, Holy, Catholic and Apostolic Church

Traditionally, from the earliest centuries of Christianity, theologians have consistently described the Church of Christ, his body, by four characteristic signs. The Church is one, holy, catholic and apostolic. Prat summarizes these signs in this way: "As the mystical body of Christ, the Church is *one*; as his bride, it is *holy*; as the temple of God, it has for its foundation the *apostles*; as the kingdom of heaven, it is *catholic* or universal."[10]

There is only one Christ and one body of Christ, the Church. There is also only one Gospel of Christ. Thus Paul could insist: "You're all one in Christ Jesus" (Gal 3:28). There is a one-ness through the one Holy Spirit, the Animator of the life of the risen Lord Jesus in us. The Church is one through the one authority empowered by Christ to his apostles and their successors, the teaching body of the Church. There is also, therefore, through the Tradition handed down by the teaching guides of the Church, one common faith that serves as an external rule and standard of belief and for living the truth. There is a unity through the basic "incorporation" into Christ of his members through the sacrament of Baptism. Christians are made into one family, "fellow citizens with the saints and members of God's household" (Eph 2:19).

Although all members are distinct individuals, as is Christ, yet in him through the Holy Spirit, as we "make every effort to maintain unity of spirit in the bond of peace," we form "one body and one Spirit, just as you were called to the one hope of your calling. One Lord, one faith, one baptism, one God and Father of us all, who is above all, through all, and in all" (Eph 4:3-6).

The Church and its members are *holy* through the union of the Church, the Bride of Christ, with him who is its Spouse.

---

[10] Prat, p. 278.

Christ's holiness — made manifest through his self-emptying unto death on the cross and by his resurrection from the dead and the release of the Holy Spirit — is shared with the bridal Church and its members. This is the eternal plan of God the Father who "chose us in Christ before the foundation of the world to be holy and blameless in his sight" (Eph 1:4).

The Church is *catholic* in its universality as was announced by the prophets of the Old Testament and by Christ's imperative to his apostles to preach the Gospel to all nations. With Christ the idea that the Jewish nation was the only nation chosen by God came to an end. All human beings have been made in the image and likeness of God (Gn 1:26-27). No one is excluded from Christ and his body, the Church. All are called to be children of the same universal Father over us all.

Thus the sign of the Church's catholicity is always and necessarily linked with the Church's universality. This adds to the call of each member of the Church to do away with any obstacle impeding the universal unity of the Church as well as to transcend any national, social, religious or individual differences that would destroy that unity in truth and love.

We can readily understand that the Church must also be grounded in the preaching of the revealed truths of Christ through his early disciples. Thus the Church is *apostolic*. Paul writes: "You were built upon a foundation of apostles and prophets, and Christ Jesus was its cornerstone" (Eph 2:20). Both Jesus and his apostles built upon the teachings of the prophets of the Old Testament, since Christ came, not to destroy, but to fulfill and perfect the law and the prophets. Through the voices of the hierarchy, the Church has passed Christ's teachings down to all subsequent generations.

Jesus sends us his Spirit that we may become living members of his body, the Church, and minister, in love and humble service, to others. This was the life of Jesus on earth, and it is the sign that we are his disciples and that he lives within us and among us. The risen Jesus is now found in his Church.

We, his members, are called to bring forth by the Spirit abundant fruit: the sign you are Christ's disciples, living his risen life, is this: "By this is my Father glorified, that you bear much fruit and become my disciples" (Jn 15:8).

7

ST. PAUL THE MYSTIC

$\Diamond$

ONE OF THE MOST difficult concepts to define is that of mysticism or simply what is a mystic. A college student, freaked out by dropping "acid," talks about his or her "mystical" experience. The yuppie business man, who sits assiduously each morning and evening for 15 minute periods of "transcendental meditation," talks to his friends of his mystical union with the Unknown. Some Protestant fundamentalists link mysticism with occultism and will have nothing to do with it. A Catholic nun sits in the lotus position and gets on her "level" to meet her healing Savior.

Yet regardless of the form, there seems to be a common element in most mysticism. Evelyn Underhill gives us an apt definition of mysticism that well applies to the mystical view of St. Paul, even though he would not have understood the term as we moderns use it:

> Mysticism is the expression of the innate yearning of the human spirit towards total harmony with the transcendental order, whatever may be the theological formula in which this order is expressed. This yearning with the great mystics gradually takes possession of the whole field of consciousness; it dominates their whole life and attains its climax in that experience called mystic union....

This desire for union and straining towards it inasmuch as they are vital and real (not purely speculative) constitute the real subject of mysticism. Through this, the human consciousness reaches its further and richest development.[1]

Paul's Use of "Mysterion"

If we impose upon Paul's writings our modern understanding of *mysticism*, we would do him a great injustice. Our usual understanding of mysticism implies a privileged experience of a union with God, the ultimate Source and Goal of all creatures. It is usually linked to ecstatic, religious experiences, filled with much sensible feeling.[2]

We have already pointed out in Chapter One that Paul had never used our term, *mysticism*, but used the adjective, *mystikos*, which for him would refer to living in the *mysteries* of the Christian faith, revealed by Christ to his disciples, including Paul, and passed down to all succeeding generations of Christians through the Church. J. Huby points out that Paul uses the word, *mystery*, 21 times to refer to being initiated into the mysteries of the "divine secret now revealed that touch on the plan of salvation of the world through Christ."[3]

Paul does not start with us human beings in our pursuit of God, but rather always focuses primarily on God's salvific plan. Such knowledge of God's divine predilection in choosing us to become participators in God's very own nature (2 P 1:4) can come only from God's gratuitousness and not from

---

[1] Evelyn Underhill, *The School of Charity and the Mystery of Sacrifice* (NY, 1956), p. 235.

[2] Cf. Joseph Huby, SJ, *Mystiques Paulinienne et Johannique* (Paris: Desclée de Brouwer & Cie, 1946), p. 7.

[3] *Ibid.*

any merit or intellectual understanding on our part. "In his love he destined us beforehand to be his adopted sons through Jesus Christ, according to the purpose and desire of his will, to the praise of the glorious grace he bestowed upon us in his Beloved" (Eph 1:5-6).

Scholars have debated for centuries whether Paul developed a mysticism influenced by the Greek cults derived from the Samothracian gods Cybele, Attis, Adonis and the Egyptian deities Isis and Osiris.[4] Paul surely was acquainted with the more popular cults since he was usually instructing Greeks who came from such religious backgrounds. He even used comparable literary forms — especially in his captivity epistles to the Ephesians and Colossians which reflect Orphic and Hermetic vocabulary.[5]

Revelation of the Mystery

Even though Paul may have used a similar term, *mysterion*, as used by the Hellenic cults, nevertheless he used the term of initiating (in Greek, *mueo*), in a completely different way than the cults used it. For Paul such an initiation into the Christian faith concerned the mysterious paths followed by God from the beginning of time unto the accomplishment of his design at the end of the world, as L. Cerfaux points out.[6] We should search to find influences upon Paul's use of the concept of mystery in Judaism's apocalyptic and wisdom literature.

---

[4] Cf. Kittel, ed., *op. cit.*, Vol. IV, art., *Mysterion*, by G. Bornkamm, p. 802 ff.

[5] On the roots and teachings of Orphism and the Hermetic literature, cf. *The Encyclopedia of Religion* (NY: Macmillan Publishing Co., 1987), Vol. 11, *Orpheus*, art. by Marcel Detienne, pp. 111-114, and Vol. 6, art. by Jean-Pierre Mahé, *Hermes Trismegistos*, pp. 287-293.

[6] L. Cerfaux, *The Christian in the Theology of St. Paul, op. cit.*, p. 483.

Knowledge of the Mystery

Paul deals with knowledge of the *mystery* as the central point in his captivity epistles. In the preceding epistles, the term is used by Paul only once or twice, meaning in a global sense the universal plan of salvation. But Paul uses the term five times in Ephesians and four times in Colossians. Here we see what Paul would understand and teach his converts by the word *mystery*.[7]

In these two epistles written in captivity in Rome, Paul uses the term, *epignosis*,[8] different from the usual word, *gnosis*, that he frequently used earlier in his two epistles to the Corinthians. This term represented for Paul a deep kind of heart-knowledge of the living mystery of God's providence, working out of our salvation in the details of our daily life. This Greek word translates quite accurately the Old Testament word, *yada*, indicating salvific knowledge involving a positive and complete response to God's call on our part.

Paul was aware of the privilege he shared with the first apostles of Jesus to preach the "mystery of Christ":

> To me, the least of all the saints, was given the grace of proclaiming to the Gentiles the unfathomable riches of Christ and to reveal for all the plan of the mystery that was hidden for ages in God, the creator of all things, so that the multi-faceted wisdom of God might now be made known through the Church to the rulers and powers in the heavens (Eph 3:8-10).

There could not be the full revelation of the mystery of God's salvific plan except through the incarnation of the Son of God in human form. Paul uses the Greek word, *photizein*,

---

[7] *Ibid.*, p. 495.
[8] Cf. the last three pages in Chapter Five, which discuss how the Holy Spirit helps us in our daily life.

to show the work of Christ through his Holy Spirit, "to bring to light," the hidden mystery of God's desire to share his divine nature with us human beings through the grace of Christ and the Spirit.[9] Paul often uses this word tied to the idea of deeper knowledge (*epignosis*) to describe the Christian being "enlightened" through Christ and his Spirit and growing from being a child in the spiritual life to full maturity in loving union with Christ. "It is Christ whom we proclaim, and we admonish and instruct everyone in all wisdom so that we'll be able to present each of them as perfect in Christ" (Col 1:28).

Paul's Preaching of the Mystery

Paul taught a mystical union of Christians in Christ and Christ in them. This differed greatly from the Asian cults' *gnosis*. Paul's mystical union is not exclusive to a limited number of initiates, but is universally open to all human beings, since God is so rich in mercy (Eph 2:4) as to send us Jesus Christ, God-Man, as our Savior. By his death and resurrection and the outpouring of the Spirit we are to be "grounded in faith and rooted in love" (Eph 3:16), and are meant to experience "Christ's love which surpasses all knowledge (*gnosis*) so that you may be filled with all God's fullness" (Eph 3:19).

Paul would insist that it is our duty to "know" the "mysteries" of our faith by our reflecting in prayerful thanksgiving on God's plan of salvation in Christ Jesus and the Holy Spirit. Christians are to be known by their "heart" knowledge (*epignosis*), their "love for one another." This loving knowledge flows in and through God's wisdom in his historical plan of salvation. By the Spirit's power and through his infused gifts of faith, hope and above all love (1 Cor 13:13), we are to grow in

---

[9] Cf. Kittel, ed., *op. cit.*, Vol. IX, art., *Phodzo,* by Hans Conzelmann, pp. 310-358.

experiencing "the richness of this glorious mystery... this *mystery* which is Christ in you, the hope of glory" (Col 1:27).

Our "straining toward the goal" (Ph 3:14) develops through our personal, experiential contact with Christ (Col 1:2; 2:6). Living in God's wisdom and the Spirit's love, we are called in Christ to live out our Baptism through a mystical death and resurrection by which we die to sin and rise to a "new life in Christ" (Col 3:4). This demands a certain praxis or ascetical lifestyle that Paul taught and lived in order to purify our hearts and minds so that they will be open to ever deeper levels of union in Christ (Gal 2:19-20).

Living in the mystery of Christ gives us the proper basis for a true Christian mysticism. Paul, as we have pointed out, never encouraged his converts to strive for any "mystical" gift that would be recognized by ecstatic feelings reserved to the "private" enjoyment of a certain few elected persons, divorced from any self-giving service to others in building up the Body of Christ.

Mystical Experiences Tied to Ministry

Let us see how Paul experienced "ecstatic" states of intense personal power as he grew in ever greater union with Christ. We will see how his personal mystical experiences came as gifts that might serve him in his efforts to extend the body of Christ through his zealous apostolate.

We, too, but perhaps not as powerfully as Paul experienced the active working of Christ and the Trinity in his life, can from time to time experience the indwelling presence and working of the Holy Spirit within us as we are grounded in the *mystery* of Christ living in us. True Christian mysticism, as outlined by Paul, must be grounded upon the love of God working in us and in our world and our response by returning God's love, living and working in Christ to build up his body through service to others.

The Primacy of Love

Any mystical phenomena, such as visions and revelations, are by their nature transitory. They do not constitute a permanent state as the Asian Gnostic cults taught. They are non-essential actual graces given by God to some individuals through the charismatic gifts of the Holy Spirit. Paul downplays them as he downplays any external claims to privilege in the body of Christ: "For in Christ Jesus neither circumcision nor uncircumcision have any meaning — what matters is faith working through love" (Gal 5:6).

Apparition of Christ to Paul on the Way to Damascus

The pivotal apparition of Christ to Paul on the road to Damascus is the beginning, not only of Paul's seemingly sudden conversion to Christ, but of Paul's mystical life in Christ. The first account we have is given to us by Luke, Paul's companion on several missionary trips and an eyewitness of his transformation in Christ:

> But Saul was still breathing threats of murder against the disciples of the Lord. He approached the high priest and asked him for letters to the synagogues in Damascus, so that if he found anyone who belonged to the Way — both men and women — he could bring them to Jerusalem in chains. Now while he was on his way, as he was approaching Damascus, suddenly a light from Heaven shone around him. As he fell to the ground he heard a voice saying to him, "Saul, Saul, why are you persecuting me?" "Who are you, Lord?" he asked. "I am Jesus, whom you are persecuting!" the voice replied. "Get up and go into the city and you'll be told what to do." The men who were traveling with him stood there speechless, for though they heard the voice they saw no one.

> Saul rose from the ground but when he opened his eyes
> he could see nothing, so they took him by the hand and
> led him into Damascus (Ac 9:1-8).

The narrative divides into two parts: the vision of Christ
to Saul (Ac 9:1-9) and a double vision of Ananias and Saul leading to Saul's cure and baptism (vv. 10-19). The importance of
this vision of Christ to Paul is seen in his references to it in his
epistles. In Gal 1:15-16 he links his predestination on the part
of God to his recognition that even then he was chosen by God
to preach to the Gentiles: "...the One who set me apart from
my mother's womb and called me through his grace was pleased
to reveal his Son to me so that I might proclaim his good news
to the Gentiles."

In this first vision that Paul had of Christ we are told of a
blinding exterior light that blazed forth and covered both Paul
and his companions and of the voice that spoke and was heard
by all of them. Yet only Paul received an interior light that suddenly changed the zealous persecutor of the early Christians in
Jerusalem and Damascus into an ardent believer in Jesus Christ
as the risen Lord and Messiah sent by God to bring salvation to
all those who would accept him.

Paul appeals in 1 Cor 9:1 to this vision to convince the
Corinthians of his legitimate claim to being an apostle equal to
the others: "Have I not seen Jesus our Lord? Are you not my
work in the Lord?" In a similar manner he refers back to this
appearance of Christ to claim his legitimacy as an apostle, personally chosen by him:

> Last of all he appeared to me as well, to one born at the
> wrong time, as it were, for I'm the least of the apostles,
> not even worthy to be called an apostle, because I per-
> secuted God's Church. But through the grace of God I
> am what I am, and the grace he gave me has not been
> without result (1 Cor 15:8).

What stands out in this vision of Christ to Paul is the suddenness of his conversion. He immediately became obedient to the Lord whom he had come to believe, through the illumination of the Holy Spirit, was truly the long-awaited Messiah. From a persecutor breathing "threats of murder" (Ac 26:10, 11) Paul becomes "… a chosen vessel to bring [Christ's] name before the Gentiles and their kings and before the sons of Israel." Christ next appears to Ananias and sends him to heal Paul of his physical blindness and to baptize him, restoring his physical sight and giving him new spiritual eyes (Ac 9:15-18).

Paul learned in this inner illumination that Jesus is alive and lives in his members. Persecuting them, Paul was persecuting the risen Lord (*Kyrios*), which term Paul would use consistently in his epistles to refer to the glorified, risen, historical Jesus who had died on the cross on Calvary but now lives on in his Church (Ph 2:10). Paul would always humbly be grateful for the complete gratuitousness of God who chose him in spite of his distorted zeal in persecuting the early followers of Jesus. Paul would recall his conversion by insisting that Christ had seized him on the road to Damascus and made him his apostle to the Gentiles (Ac 22:4-5; 26:9-11; Gal 1:13-14; 1 Cor 15:9; 1 Tm 1:12-16).[10]

Paul realized at Damascus that he could not belong to Christ without belonging to his body, the Church (Ac 9:4-5). Huby well describes the effects on Paul of his sudden conversion:

> To respond to this love of Christ, St. Paul had sacrificed all the advantages he received from his race, his family, his social situation within the heart of Judaism.[11]

---

[10] Cf. Jerome Crowe, CP, *The Acts* (Wilmington, DE: Michael Glazier, Inc., 1979), pp. 61ff.

[11] Huby, p. 112.

Paul would compare the advantages he had enjoyed within the cradle of Judaism with what he would begin to receive in following Christ:

> But whatever I had gained from all this, I have come to consider it loss for the sake of Christ. In fact, I consider everything to be loss for the sake of the surpassing greatness of knowing Christ Jesus my Lord. For his sake I've cast everything aside and regard it as so much rubbish so that I'll gain Christ and be found in him, having no righteousness of my own based on observance of the Torah but only that righteousness which comes through faith in Christ.

> … My goal is to know him and the power of his resurrection, to understand the fellowship of his sufferings and become conformed to his death in the hope of somehow attaining resurrection from the dead (Ph 3:7-11).

Other Visions and Revelations of the Lord

In 2 Cor 12:1, Paul tells the Corinthians about other visions and revelations of the Lord that he received.[12] He adds in verse 7 that, because of "these extraordinary revelations" he had received from the Lord, he was given "a thorn in the flesh… to keep me from getting puffed up." In this text (2 Cor 12:2-4) Paul relates the outstanding rapture he experienced fourteen years earlier as he was swept up into the "Third Heaven," to Paradise.

The setting of this narrative has to be understood, for Paul is giving the Corinthians and all of us a most valuable lesson concerning ecstatic mysticism as compared to Pauline mysticism that is sealed by loving service to the community. Paul's

---

[12] I am indebted to J. Huby, *op.cit.*, for the many texts he provides of Paul's visions and revelations.

opponents in Corinth, who eagerly sought out mystical, ecstatic experiences, considered such mystical experiences as a positive proof of God's favor and election. Paul uses parody to correct their thinking by boasting as a fool about some of his own mystical experiences, especially the rapture he experienced of being lifted up into Paradise.

Such boasting is for Paul foolishness. It is the only time Paul uses the third person to hide, in humility, the fact that he is the subject of such an experience. He would end by giving the true criterion of an authentic apostle: to be of service in building up the Christian community, the Church (cf. 2 Cor 8:10; 1 Cor 6:12).

Mocking the tones of his opponents' certitude that the human soul ascends to heaven, Paul states that he does not know whether the soul or the person ascended but he would rather leave such knowledge to God. Francis T. Fallon in his commentary on this text presents the customary understanding of "heaven" in the time of Paul:

> In accord with a customary conception of that era, there were considered to be three heavens: the heaven of the planets, the heaven of the fixed stars, and the final heaven in which God resided.[13]

Paul has the man snatched up to Paradise, a part of the Third Heaven in which the blessed were thought to dwell after their death or after the final judgment (vs. 3). Paul in substance is telling his opponents, influenced by Hellenistic, Gnostic syncretism prevalent among many of the Greek Jews in Corinth at that time, that he had heard the divine secrets which were communicated to God's elect. But then he states that these secrets cannot be told. Paul does not, unlike his opponents, report what ineffable secrets he has heard. He does this to convince the

---

[13] Francis T. Fallon, *Two Corinthians* (Wilmington, DE: Michael Glazier, Inc., 1980), p. 105.

Corinthians that the claim to visions by his opponents of true apostleship proves nothing. As the wise fool, Paul wishes to make the only proper boast about himself when he boasts paradoxically about his weakness.

Paul tells his opponents that he will not boast of that person who had such ecstatic visions; but of his true self, with all his "weakness," and of his true claim to being Christ's apostle he will boast. Huby makes a concrete application of Paul's evaluation of such ecstatic visions and the true authentic sign of Christian holiness when he appeals to the Church's pronouncement on the sanctity of a member to be canonized. "When the Church pronounces on the sanctity of a member, it founds its judgment on the heroism of virtues and not on extraordinary favors, as visions and revelations. But the signs of love of God and neighbor developed to a supreme degree, the works and trials endured for Christ with heroic courage, in such does God primarily manifest the power of his grace."[14]

Meeting God in Paul's Dreams

We find many accounts of how God communicated to Paul ways to save his life or to be more effective in his preaching. Acts 18:9-10 mentions how Christ appeared to him in a dream around the years 51-52. This occurred during Paul's first stay in Corinth. He habitually preached on the Sabbath in Jewish synagogues but frequently received only violent opposition from his hearers. And so, at one point, he decided to turn all his attention to evangelize the Gentiles.

> Then the Lord said to Paul in a vision one night, "Don't be afraid! Speak and don't be silent, for I am with you. No one will attack or try to harm you, for I have many people in this city" (Ac 18:9-10).

---

[14] Huby, *op. cit.*, p. 122, tr. my own.

We note that the vision took place at night. Can we believe it was a vision in a dream or a vision while Paul was praying one night? It could surely be a dream similar to those found in the Old and New Testaments (e.g., Gn 31:11 to Jacob; Mt 1:20 to Joseph). Not only in Judaism and Christianity, but in almost all religions, dreams have been considered a very common way which God uses to communicate with human beings.

Other visions in dreams during night are recorded. After Paul had been arrested in Jerusalem and was summoned before the Sanhedrin (Ac 23:11), the Lord appeared to Paul to console him: "Take courage. For just as you've given witness on my behalf in Jerusalem, so too must you bear witness in Rome."

Paul himself writes to the Galatians how seventeen years after his conversion, the Spirit inspired him to travel to Jerusalem to meet with the leaders there. "I went because of a revelation. I met privately with those held in repute and set out for them the gospel that I preach among the Gentiles, lest I should somehow be running or have run in vain" (Gal 2:2).

The interventions of the Spirit guiding Paul to know the will of God in certain concrete details of his apostolate should not be limited to some occasional happenings. As we have pointed out several times in Chapters Five and Six, Paul was totally aware that without the constant help of the Spirit he would be unable to spread the Gospel to the Gentiles. "For our proclamation of the good news didn't come to you in words alone but also with power, with the Holy Spirit, and with complete certainty" (1 Th 1:5).

The Holy Spirit guides Paul in his preaching and in his travels through interior graces accompanied by signs and wonders. Paul's power to heal and perform miracles, added to the charismatic gifts of prophecy and *glossolalia* (speaking in tongues), were not only witnessed in the churches of Corinth and Galatia, but wherever Paul preached. Paul not only received from the Spirit the gift of prophecy, which precisely meant for

Paul to preach in the Spirit's wisdom and power, but also inner knowledge of practical concerns on how to apply the Gospel he preached to the pastoral and administrative needs of the churches he guided.

Paul often appeals to the fact that he always followed the Tradition handed down by the first early apostles who had received the fundamental teachings directly from Christ. But Paul, also under the inspiration of the Holy Spirit, made known certain truths which the apostolic Tradition did not explicitly hand down. He was aware that he had been better trained in the rabbinical school in Jerusalem under Rabbi Gamaliel in the Old Testament teachings, especially the prophecies, than the other twelve, and so was in a better position to interpret them.

Paul clearly tells the Galatians that the Gospel he preached to the Gentiles came not from any human teacher but through the revelations of Jesus Christ:

> I want you to know, brothers, that the good news I proclaimed is not a human gospel, for I didn't receive it from any man nor was I taught it — I received it through a revelation of Jesus Christ (Gal 1:11-12).

Paul received much from the common teachings of the apostles and elders in Jerusalem, especially concerning the doctrine of the resurrection of Jesus and his presence in the Eucharist: "So whether it was me or them, this is what we proclaimed and this is what you believed" (1 Cor 15:11). But what Paul could claim came to him, not by human teachers, i.e., from the apostles, but directly from Christ, is Paul's mystical vision of the mystery of God's salvific plan through Jesus Christ. This salvific plan concerned the new life, especially in the Eucharist, that makes us one with the risen Lord who fashions us through the unifying gift of love, the Holy Spirit, into Christ's Body, the Church. Paul testifies that Christ and the Holy Spirit inspired him with this insight through a personal and immediate revelation: "For I received from the Lord what I handed down to you, that on the night he was betrayed the Lord Jesus took bread, and after blessing it he broke it and said, 'This is my body that is for you. Do this in remembrance of me'" (1 Cor 11:23-25).

On the ship carrying Paul to Rome, an angel of the Lord appeared to Paul during a violent storm. He was assured that all the passengers aboard would be safe, but the ship would sink (Ac 27:22-26). We can also interpret as an apparition in the form of a dream the vision Paul received in his second voyage around 50 AD. Luke describes the vision given to Paul one night in Troas: "That night Paul had a vision: a man from Macedonian was standing there imploring him, 'Come over to Macedonia and help us'" (Ac 16:9). We are told by Luke that as a result of this vision, "we immediately sought passage to Macedonia, having concluded that God had called us to proclaim the good news to them" (vs. 10).

Guided by the Inspirations of the Spirit

Paul continually exhorted his converts to be open to the guidance of the Holy Spirit: "So, too, no one knows what God intends except the Spirit of God. But the Spirit we have received is not the spirit of this world but the Spirit that comes from God and enables us to know what it is that God has freely bestowed upon us" (1 Cor 2:11-12). To be inwardly attentive, especially in time of deep prayer, to the subtle inspirations of the Holy Spirit was one of the great means Paul found helpful to him in receiving communications from God.

During Paul's second apostolic voyage, he passed through Phrygia and Galatia, eager to penetrate the rich and populated province of Asia with Ephesus its capital. But "the Holy Spirit had forbidden them to preach the word in the province of Asia. When they reached Mysia, they tried to go on to Bithynia, but the Spirit of Jesus wouldn't allow them to, so they went on through Mysia and came down to Troas" (Ac 16:6-8).

We will discuss in the next chapter how Paul was especially taught by Christ concerning the end of this world and the parousia or full manifestation of Christ in and through the members of his body who will "recapitulate" all things by completing God's eternal plan of salvation.

8

THE END OF THE WORLD

———— ◊ ————

We have highlighted Paul's constant emphasis on the indwelling presence of Christ through the power of his resurrection. Our whole Christian faith, as we have earlier stressed, hinges on the resurrection of the body of the Lord. If it had not taken place our faith would be vain, in the sense of being empty, for Christ would not, ontologically, have reversed the sentence of death. He would not have rescued us human beings from our estrangement from God. We would not have had restored to us the "spirit," that is, God's own life.

To live in God through his full humanity, to live the divine life of the Spirit — that is why Christ had to rise and die no more. It is true that before his resurrection, he personally enjoyed the fullness of God's divine life. After his resurrection, however, he possessed it in his role as our living and life-giving head. He passed from a carnal existence to one completely spiritual, *pneumatic*. In this new modality or manner of existing, Jesus Christ could transcend all space and time and apply to us the merits of his sacrifice, the shedding of his blood, whereby we could draw near again to God.

In Christ's death, God condemned sin in the flesh (Rm 8:3). The power of sin was broken. The resurrection of Christ is uniquely important because his new and glorious life makes him the new Adam, the Lord of the universe, capable under this new modality of bestowing upon us the same life of the Spirit by making us daughters and sons of his heavenly Father.

In this chapter we want to examine the impact of faith in the risen Lord upon Paul's eschatological teachings, concerning the end of the world as we know it.

The Cosmic Christ

Eschatology in Christian creeds and theology is the study from Scripture and the teachings of the Church that deals with the *goal* of God's plan of salvation and the *telos* or end of our earthly journey.[1] Prat describes what Christian eschatology embraces:

> Under the comprehensive name of *eschatology* are often designated death and the intermediate state, the *parousia* with its precedent signs, the resurrection, the judgment, the retribution of the good and the wicked, and the consummation of all things... which includes, besides individual destinies, the final lot of humanity and the ultimate transformation of the universe.[2]

Paul's emphasis on the eschatological themes, as we see so strongly presented by him in his early epistles, the First and Second Epistles to the Thessalonians, tends to diminish over time. Paul in his later letters in captivity, Colossians and Ephesians, highlights Christ's redemption of the entire created universe in his cosmic role to *recapitulate* or *reestablish* them in their lost unity under his own headship.

We should first, therefore, start with Paul's doctrine of

[1] Cf. Kittel, ed., *op. cit.*, Vol. II, art., *Eschatos*, pp. 697-698.
[2] Prat, Vol. II, *op. cit.*, p. 352.

Christ's universal redemption of all that God has created before we examine in detail his specific teachings of the end times. The indwelling Spirit that Christ sends us, not only imparts to our souls the ontological life of God through grace, but he exerts his influence on our bodies as well (Rm 8:11). But tied intrinsically to our material bodies, that are destined to a future redemption through a spiritual resurrection, is the whole universe.

Paul ties the destiny of all creation to our human sanctification. He imagines the created universe waiting for the manifestation of the children of God. The material world was made subject to *vanity*, that is, was misused by the pride of Adam and Eve. It was human beings who cast the universe into the "slavery to corruption" (Rm 8:21) by sin. The whole of creation is, like a mother in agony before giving birth, groaning and laboring in pain "until now" (Rm 8:22).

Christ's dominion over the entire universe is pictured in Paul's epistles to the Colossians and Ephesians. Among these Asiatic Christians there was the influence of a Gnostic cosmology, filled with a morbid craze for speculation about heavenly spirits and powers. False teachers maintained that angelic powers, intermediate beings between God and human beings, were also causes of creation (Col 1:19; 2:9; 1:15-17). They could exert great power over the birth and destiny of human beings and were to be worshipped.

The gravity of the heresy consisted in the implicit denial of Christ's unique position as the sole mediator and redeemer of the human race. For this reason Paul stresses the uniqueness of Christ in his dual role as mediator and redeemer. In Colossians 1:15-20 Paul stresses that all things are created and are preserved in their being through and for him. "He is before all things, and in him all things hold together" (vs. 16). Earlier, in his Epistle to the Philippians, Paul had hinted at Christ's universal dominion over all creation:

He will transform our lowly bodies so that they'll have the same form as his glorious body, by means of the power that enables him to subject everything to himself (Ph 3:21).

We see in these texts clear examples of Paul's use of a cosmic setting, based on the cosmology of his times, to relate in a more dramatic way the full extent of Christ's dominion over all creation, visible and invisible. All creatures were created to be under the dominion of Christ. They had lost their proper orientation and had to be reconciled by the same Christ, who is both their exclusive beginning and final end. Their rebellion was put down, but not completely destroyed. This work of reconciliation still goes on in the universe. C.K. Barrett summarizes Christ's cosmic redemptive power:

> The ordered universe is now disordered, and has reached such pitch of rebellion that he who is the image of the Invisible God-Wisdom, Word, a Torah, Urmensch, Microcosmos, call him what you will, can only retrieve the situation by shedding his blood and overcoming the power of death by experiencing it. This means that the work of the heavenly Man can be apprehended not in creation as it now exists, but only in the process of redemption.[3]

Only in Second Corinthians does Paul develop in greater detail the relationship between God and Christians in the reconciliation of the universe to the Father effected through Christ. Our human role as Christ's ambassadors (2 Cor 5:17) is enunciated in the ministry of reconciliation by preaching the Gospel to all creatures. This is a greater responsibility than merely preaching to other human beings. Our ministry of co-reconciliation with Christ must touch even the cosmos (2 Cor 5:17-21).

We see Paul's urgency of proclaiming the Gospel, not only

---

[3] C.K. Barrett, *From First Adam to Last: A Study in Pauline Theology* (NY: Scribner, 1962), p. 87.

in word, but in deed. Christ's message must be proclaimed to the ends of the earth in every generation. Even the cosmos must come under the influence of Christ and his message. The cosmos is groaning until the fullness of time when human beings will live by the message of the Divine Word and thus cooperate in bringing the whole universe to its fullness.

The Fullness or "Pleroma"

To understand what Paul means by Christ's reestablishing all things in their fullness when he will come again at the end of the world (*parousia*), we must first look at the meaning of the word, *pleroma*, fullness.[4] In general this term is used in Paul's epistles to mean "that which fills," referring to "content," e.g., 1 Cor 10:25. It is often used to express, "full measure," or "completion" or "full maturity."

Paul uses *pleroma* in five important texts in his two captivity letters, thus giving to it a specialized, technical meaning.

1. "For in him all the *fullness* was pleased to dwell" (Col 1:19). Here there is question of a fixed abode. God wills that the fullness be in Christ in order that he might reconcile and pacify all things. In this text, *pleroma* could not refer to the fullness of the divine essence which Christ possesses as God, nor is there any question of it referring to the Church as the fullness dwelling in him. Paul means that Christ, through his redemptive work and by means of his present glorious resurrectional life, assumes in himself not only regenerated humanity, which is his body, but also the whole cosmos which becomes a new creation, at least potentially, to form the framework of this body.

2. "For in Christ dwells the fullness of divinity in bodily

---

[4] Cf. Kittel, ed., *op. cit.*, Vol. VI, art., *Pleroma*, by G. Delling, pp. 298-305.

form, and in him you reach completion; he is the head of every ruler and power" (Col 2:9-10). Paul says that through the incarnation Christ has taken upon himself a body and now the fullness of the Godhead has been localized in this Body-Person, Christ. Christians find fulfillment in him because they exist now as new creatures in Christ who fills them with his own divine resurrected life. They come into contact with his divine fullness when they become incorporated into him by means of Baptism.

3. "...that you may be filled with all God's *fullness*" (Eph 3:19). Paul uses the cosmic dimensions of the term *pleroma* to apply it to the one great reality that is ever before his eyes in his letter to the Ephesians, namely, the Church. Christians, by becoming more perfect, build up the fullness of God in the Church. God's fullness exists perfectly within the immanent action of the Trinitarian life, but now it must be brought to a fullness in the Church on earth.

4. "He has put all things under his feet and has given him as head over all things to the Church, which is his body, the fullness of the One who fills all things in their totality" (Eph 1:22-23). Here we see Christ is completed in his mission as Savior and Redeemer by the members of the Church who continue and prolong his work through time and space until the end of this world. It is Christ who supplies the members through the power of the Holy Spirit with all necessary graces.

5. "... until we all attain to the unity of faith and knowledge of the Son of God, to mature manhood, to the extent of Christ's full stature" (Eph 4:13). Again the fullness of Christ is coextensive with the body of Christ, the Church. Christ individually, in his risen and glorious existence in Heaven, enjoys fullness as head of the Church. His body, however, made of all human beings who are in the process of being saved, is still in the process of formation on this earth.

Thus we can say that *pleroma* for Paul, at least in his epistles to the Colossians and Ephesians, where he is especially concerned with presenting Christ in his cosmic dimensions, refers to a multiple fullness. Christ in his risen Body-Person, possesses the fullness of the Godhead. Yet precisely through the same glorious new existence of the Body-Person, Jesus Christ, is he able to communicate this same divine life to us human beings who are forming his body, the Church.

This formation goes on without ceasing in the universe until the end of time. Christ is conceived not only as the chief and head that commands his body, but also as the principle that nourishes this body. Through his sacramental union of grace with individual members who form his body, the Church, Christ extends his influence to the entire universe. The cosmos or created world is being redeemed through Christ and thus is arriving gradually at its goal of fullness, which is God himself.

"Parousia" or the Second Coming of Christ

Having established the cosmic dimension of Christ the Recapitulator who fulfills God's plan of salvation by bringing all of creation into completion, we can examine Paul's specific teachings on the Second Coming at the end of the times, which in Christian eschatology is expressed by the Greek word, *parousia.*

The word *parousia* is usually used to express a presence or a coming of a person. In the Hellenic period in which Paul was writing, this word had a technical meaning, both political and religious. It denoted the triumphal entry of rulers, kings, emperors, high ranking magistrates, and religious leaders into a city. Because sovereigns were treated as gods and gods were treated as rulers, the two senses melded into each other. Paul undoubtedly had such a triumphal entry of a sovereign in mind in the description he gives of Christ's victorious return to earth at the end of time.[5]

---

[5] Kittel, ed., *op. cit.*, Vol. V, art., *Parousia*, by A. Oepke, pp. 858-871.

> The Lord himself will come down from Heaven and is-
> sue a command, with an archangel's voice and a blast
> from God's trumpet. Those who died in Christ will rise
> first, then we who are living, who remain, will be caught
> up into the clouds with them to meet the Lord in the air,
> and so we'll always be with the Lord (1 Th 4:16-17).

It is clearly in his two epistles written c. 50 AD that Paul presents his most skeletal view of Christ's Second Coming. Why this concern developed in the church of Thessalonica can perhaps be traced to a misconception among the faithful of that church that through Baptism a Christian entered the Kingdom of final glory here and now. This led to an erroneous disregard on the part of the faithful for living their normal lives of work and evangelization. They spent their time awaiting Christ's coming in glory and the immanent end of this material world.[6] Paul, even though he himself believed that he would be alive at Christ's coming, vigorously corrected the Thessalonians' belief regarding the immediacy of the coming (*parousia*; see 2 Th 2:12).

The Event of the Parousia

Sometimes Paul, especially in his two epistles to the Thessalonians, seems to hold with those Christians the imminence of the Second Coming of Christ in glory. At other times, especially in his more mature writings to the Colossians and Ephesians, Paul already realizes that even for him in his prison cell in Rome he would not see the final coming of Christ. He realistically knew that the evangelization of the Gentile "world" would not be accomplished in his lifetime.

Yet Paul never loses sight of the great event of the *parousia*

---

[6] Cf. James M. Reese, OSFS, *1 and 2 Thessalonians* (Wilmington, DE: Michael Glazier, Inc., 1979), pp. xiv-xvi.

since it was a basic teaching of Jesus in the Gospels and among the apostles that such a Second Coming of Christ would herald the fulfillment of all world history. "He made known to us the mystery of his will, according to the purpose he displayed in Christ, as a plan for the fullness of time — to bring all things together in Christ, things in heaven and on earth" (Eph 1:9-10).

As we have seen throughout all the preceding chapters, Paul preached the immanent, indwelling presence of Christ, an already hidden and mystical *parousia* experienced daily by the early Christians. The second *parousia* would be the full day that would follow the breaking dawn of the "new creation."

Such faith in the intimate life in Christ already lived by Christians allowed Paul to move between two different time spans, between the *chronos*, the uncompleted time in which we struggle against sin and death, and the "new time," or *kairos*, which is the basis of our living in the salvation of the risen Lord.

The "Second Coming" and the final triumph of Christ in and through his body, the Church, is a matter of great hope and desire on Paul's part and all the early Christians as they eagerly sought to live in the excitement of the fullness of their shared glory with Christ the King and Lord of the universe. Such hopeful expectancy enabled Christians to resist the evil temptations of the world and bring under captivity and in obedience to Jesus Christ every thought and every imagination (2 Cor 10:5).

Paul exhorts Titus to teach his converts to eagerly look forward to the full triumph of Christ in his Second Coming as they put on the mind of Christ in their daily living:

> For the grace of God has appeared with salvation for all men, teaching us to reject impiety and worldly passions and to live sober, upright, and godly lives in this present age as we await our blessed hope — the appearance in glory of our great God and of our Savior Christ Jesus. He gave himself for us to redeem us from all wickedness and

to purify for himself a people eager for good works (Tt 2:11-14).

The Resurrection of the Dead

The belief that there will be as a part of the *parousia* and the end of the world the resurrection of all the dead is taught in all the early Christian creeds as well as in Paul's writings. The Apostles' Creed professes: "I believe… in the resurrection of the body and life everlasting." Christ's resurrection is the anticipation of the resurrection of Christians. Paul teaches that Christ has risen from the dead as the "first fruits of those who have fallen asleep" (1 Cor 15:20), and insists on our full sharing in his glorious, risen life when he comes again in his final *parousia*:

> For just as in Adam all men die, so too in Christ they'll also come to life again. Each will be raised in the proper order — Christ the first fruits, then at his coming those who belong to Christ will rise. Then the end will come, when he'll deliver the Kingdom to his God and Father, when he'll do away with every ruler, authority, and power. For Christ must reign until he's put all his enemies under his feet. The last enemy to be done away with will be death (1 Cor 15:22-25).

Here we see Paul writing to his Christian converts and saying to them that they will rise again in glory to share Christ's triumph over sin and death if they have but cooperated in overcoming sin in their own lives. For non-Christians the resurrection of the dead as universally applied to all human beings means for Paul a potential sharing, depending upon their cooperation in conquering evil in this present life.

Characteristics of the Resurrected Body

In 1 Cor 15, Paul seeks to answer the Greek converts as to what kind of a body human beings will have in the resurrection. Paul says almost nothing about what happens to the soul when separated from the body. Yet he seeks to remove from the minds of the Greek Christians any thought of a radical separation of the body and soul by presenting them with the holistic views of his Semitic, religious training. The Greeks were brought up to see the soul as the essence of the human person while the body had meaning only as an instrument to purify the soul.

To his Greek Corinthian converts, Paul's teaching on the resurrection of the body seemed to be a contradiction. Cerfaux highlights Paul's understanding of "Spirit" and "spiritual" in order to explain his faith vision of the resurrection of the body:

> For St. Paul the idea of the Spirit is primarily "religious," and he sees the Spirit as a fundamental "quality" of God. The "spiritual" man is the man who attains contact with God through his participation in God's Spirit.... As the resurrection concerns the body, which must not only be reanimated, but enter into the "spiritual" sphere, we can say that the resurrected body is "spiritual." It will still be a body, retaining the whole of its corporeal nature, except anything which prevents it from participating in divinity (1 Cor 15:50). This, then, is the meaning of 1 Cor 15.[7]

The Last Judgment and Retribution

Building on Jewish eschatology and the apocalyptic literature of his time, Paul offers nothing original to the two basic beliefs of Judaism, namely, that there will be a general judg-

---

[7] L. Cerfaux, *The Christian in the Theology of St. Paul, op. cit.*, pp. 181-182.

ment of angels and all human beings at the end of the world accompanied by a just retribution and reward for the good or evil done before the end of time. Thus Paul insisted on a universal judgment based upon the works of angels and human beings:

> For all of us will have to appear before the judgment seat of Christ where each will receive either good or evil, depending on what we did while in the body (2 Cor 5:10; cf. Rm 2:16; 14:10; Ac 17:31).

Transformation of the Universe

Paul breaks away from Jewish eschatology with its emphasis, as we find in Peter's second epistle, on the annihilation of the entire material world. "On that day the heavens will disappear with a roar; the elements will be consumed by fire, and the earth and everything done on it will be found out" (2 P 3:10). It is perhaps Paul's most creative insight that extends the glorification of Christ through his divinizing Spirit to the glorification of Christians in the *parousia* and to present to the Father a created universe renewed through the agency of Jesus Christ and the Holy Spirit.

This "new creation" will be the dwelling place of the saints in God's Kingdom. Isaiah had centuries earlier prophesied the state of harmony that would exist between human beings and the cosmos when both would be at peace with each other and find all things in Christ. Human beings would be the masters of the created, God's true stewards and co-creators in and through the indwelling Trinity, to bring about the universe as God had intended, to reflect his infinite beauty and glory (Is 11:6, 8, 19; cf. also Ezk 34:25).

For Paul our redemption and glorification is inextricably tied up with the glorification of the world as a total unit. As man's first fall had cosmic repercussions, so too Christ's glorification and that of all those who would put on Christ, would share with the cosmos their "new creation" (2 Cor 5:17). Paul writes:

> Creation awaits the revelation of the sons of God with eager anticipation, for creation was subjected to futility, not of its own will but because of the one who made it subject, with the hope that creation itself would be freed from its slavery to corruption and be brought to the glorious freedom of the children of God (Rm 8:19-21).

The Semitic mind — and Paul follows the same thinking — conceived human beings and the material world in which we live as a unit, a community of interrelated beings on linear march to their fulfillment or completion. God never creates to destroy, but only to bring greater and greater complexity out of his infinite perfections into a unity through the synergistic cooperation of human beings with the cosmic Christ and the Holy Spirit.

In the final attainment of the end toward which all creation was moving there would be two distinct parts of Christ's victory that are even now *in via* or in process to be accomplished but only in the *parousia*. All creation, that is now subject to "vanity" whose rule is corruption, will be liberated and transformed into harmonious submission of service according to the mind of God. Then all creatures will contribute to the full glory of God that comes only from all created beings operating fully as God had intended.

This will be the cosmic act of deliverance from corruption. It is intimately bound up with the first part of Christ's victory in the *parousia*, that is, the deification of human beings into daughters and sons of God "by participation" in God's very own nature (2 P 1:4).[8]

---

[8] Cf. my work, *The Cosmic Christ: From Paul to Teilhard* (NY: Sheed & Ward, 1968), pp. 17-70.

Transmission of the Kingdom to the Father

Paul in his first epistle to the Corinthians describes the ultimate goal of God's *mysterion* or the completion of God's
salvific plan for all of his creatures around the theme of Christ,
the Redeemer and Savior, who will bring all of creation back
to the ultimate King, the heavenly Father.[9] The whole cosmos
is one with the destiny of human beings. All will be brought
back by Christ, Victor and Redeemer, and the Holy Spirit to its
Maker and Final End, the heavenly Father. Paul summarizes this
truth concisely by tying up the relationship of all things to Christ,
and of Christ transmitting all to God:

> Then the end will come, when he'll deliver the Kingdom
> to his God and Father, when he'll do away with every
> ruler, authority, and power. For Christ must reign until
> he's put all his enemies under his feet. The last enemy
> to be done away with will be death, for "God has put
> everything under his feet" (Ps 110:1 and Ps 8:7).... When
> everything is made subject to him, then the Son himself
> will be subjected to the One who subjected everything
> to the Son, so that God will be all in all (1 Cor 15:24-28).

The reason why the faithful members of Christ's Body must
wait for the Second Coming of Christ in the *parousia* in order
to enjoy full resurrection in glory in and through Christ is, therefore, seen in this text to be due to the fact that Christ's mission
to bring salvation and redemption to his members in his Body
had not yet been accomplished. Even though Christ was exalted by the Father in glory by his resurrection, yet he must
completely annihilate all evil powers, typified by Paul's use of
the symbol of death, i.e., any power or force that obstructs the
full manifestation of divine life through Christ and the Holy Spirit
(1 Cor 15:24).

---

[9] Cf. Cerfaux, *The Christian...*, *op. cit.*, pp. 218-219.

Only then will Christ in the end times in his Second Coming be able to present the Kingdom to God. In this passage (v. 24) Paul well expresses this in a masterful way as Jerome Murphy-O'Connor, O.P., states:

> The subordination of Christ, precisely as "Son," to God could not be expressed with greater clarity and is in total accord with the stress on his humanity in verse 21.[10]

God Is All In All

In his writing Paul seeks to answer the many questions his early disciples were posing to him or Timothy or Titus who relayed them to him for some solution. Paul exhorts his disciple, Timothy, possibly in charge of the churches in Ephesus: "Avoid foolish and ignorant debates, for you know that they breed quarrels" (2 Tm 2:23). Surely Paul's patience must have been tried by the "carnal minded" questions presented by some of his early Christian converts about what kind of a body they would have in the life to come, what heaven would be like compared to our life on this earth, what would happen to the damned, etc. We would hardly consider Paul to be what we would call today a "speculative theologian."

As we have seen throughout this book Paul is obsessed with the mystery of Christ as risen and dwelling within all Christians. He is content that Christians accept the truth that Jesus Christ is truly the Son of God from all eternity (Ph 2:6) and for all of us he died. He was raised from the dead and now lives gloriously with the Father and Holy Spirit. Yet he also lives among us and in each of us members of his body, the Church, and gives us already a participation in his resurrection, "Thus

---

[10] Jerome Murphy-O'Connor, OP, *1 Corinthians* (Wilmington, DE: Michael Glazier Inc., 1979), p. 143.

you too should consider yourselves dead to sin and living for God in Christ Jesus" (Rm 6:11).

Of those who have already died physically "so too in Christ they'll also come to life again" (1 Cor 15:22). Life after death will continue and we shall have a resurrected body, depending on how we have died to sin and have lived in Christ's "new creation" that will allow each person to be "spiritualized" and live, not with a material body, but as a spiritualized, unique person, living on the three levels: as an embodied spiritual being, as an ensouled person, and as an enspirited individual.

For Paul to say more is not possible since it remains hidden in God's *mysterion*, his eternal plan of salvation. Our present minds cannot even fathom what the life to come will be like when the "old" is dead and the "new" is alive in Christ (2 Cor 5:17). Paul only offers a share in the overwhelming joy and hope that are his already. "Rejoice always" (1 Th 5:17). "Rejoice in the Lord always. I say it again: rejoice" (Ph 4: 4).

Paul can bear all trials and tribulation since he lives in the strength of the risen Lord, who is his total strength in all of his infirmities (2 Cor 12:9; 2 Cor 4:17). No person and no sufferings, not even death itself, can ever separate us from the love of God, which comes to us in Christ Jesus our Lord (Rm 8:39). With an apophatic response of a knowledge that surpasses all human understanding, Paul encourages all of us as we move closer to the third millennium of Christianity to get "to know Christ's love which surpasses all knowledge, so that you may be filled with all God's fullness" (Eph 3:19).

If we were to inquire of Paul what must we still know about the life to come and the Second Coming of the Lord Jesus, I believe he would again repeat to us what he wrote to the group of Corinthians who wanted him to explain the "mystery" of God's salvation in an intellectually sophisticated way suited to their inflated rational pride:[11]

---

[11] *Ibid.*, p. 19.

But as it is written:

What eye has not seen nor ear heard,
what the human heart has not conceived,
that God has prepared for those who love him (1 Cor 2:9).

As a fitting conclusion to this final chapter, I would like
to offer a quote from Karl Rahner who beautifully summarizes
what we have discussed in this chapter, namely, how the world
is not blindly hurtling itself into aimless expansion, a mass of
heterogeneity, but is being moved by Christ to the Father that
God may be "all in all":

> Here we must remember that the world is a unity in which
> everything is linked together with everything else. When
> anyone grasps a portion of the world as a whole for his
> own life's history, at one and the same time he takes upon
> himself the world as a whole for his personal environ-
> ment. Thus it would not be extravagant, as long as it was
> done with prudence, to conceive the evolution of the
> world as an orientation toward Christ, and to represent
> the various stages of this ascending movement as culmi-
> nating in him as their apex. The only danger to be avoided
> is the suggestion that such evolution is an ascent which
> the world accomplishes by forces which are wholly its
> own. If what St. Paul says in Colossians 1:15 is true and
> not softened by some moralistic interpretation, if further-
> more the world as a whole, including therefore its physi-
> cal reality, is actually in process of reaching in and through
> Christ that final state in which God is all in all, then the
> line of thought we are developing here cannot be en-
> tirely false.[12]

---

[12] Karl Rahner, *Theological Investigations*, Vol. I (Baltimore: Helicon Press, 1960),
p. 165.

GLOSSARY

— ◊ —

Agapan; **Agapé**: In Paul's writings the verb and noun refer to living in unselfish love for God and neighbor through the Holy Spirit's infused gift of love (1 Cor 13:4-13). Such love is the fulfillment of the two great commandments: to love God with our whole heart and soul and mind; and to love our neighbor as we love ourselves (Rm 13:9-10).

Alpha: The first letter of the Greek alphabet referring in the New Testament to Christ, the preexistent Son of God in whom all creatures have their being.

Anakephaloiosis: Paul uses this word in Eph 1:9-10 to describe Christ's role assigned in the decree of his heavenly Father, namely, that when the fullness of time had arrived, God would gather all creation both in heaven and on earth under one head, Christ. Commentators offer a variety of possible meanings but "reestablish" seems to be the best translation. We can accept this to mean that Christ will restore the world's lost unity under his own headship.

Aphtharsia: Meaning "incorruptibility" and therefore "immortality." Paul and the Eastern Fathers starting with Irenaeus used this word to refer to the divine Trinitarian life that is shared as grace in the divinization process that Jesus Christ and his Spirit bring about, making us "participators in God's very own nature" (2 P 1:4).

Askein: To practice or to exercise. In Attic Greek it refers to the exercise of the body or to the practice of an art. Paul uses this word and many related terms to describe the spiritual combat Christians must enter into to uproot the unspiritual forces within and around us that would destroy God's divine life within us.

129

Baptizein: For Paul it refers to the initiation rite by immersion in water which symbolizes our death to sin and our rising to new life in Christ. It implies a complete conversion to Jesus Christ. This rite brings about our insertion into an objective, real union of life with Christ risen. It brings about remission of sins and our sharing in the new creation.

Charis: Translated in Paul's writings as "grace." He groups such gratuitous gifts and calls them *charisma* or *charismata*. These graces are gifts to us to build up the Body of Christ.

Chronos: This refers according to Paul to the historical time that begins for each human person at the moment of his or her conception and ends with that person's last moment of life on earth. With Christ's resurrection, salvific time (*kairos*) intersected our historical time bringing with it the promise and the pledge of our ultimate victory over sin and death.

Ekklesia: This Greek word translates the Hebrew word, *Qahal*, and means "the called out people of God." Paul uses this term in reference to a local church as well as the universal Church. It refers to all Christians bonded together by the same faith and sacraments, especially Baptism and the Eucharist, who live in obedience to the bishops and presbyters empowered to teach Christ's revelation with his authority.

Elpis: The Greek for "hope." Paul insists hope is built upon faith in God's fidelity and convenantual love and always implies a confident expectancy for what is not yet possessed, but promised in the future by God in Christ Jesus.

Epekteinomenos: Paul uses the analogy of a runner in the stadium who strives (lit. "stretches forward") to reach the goal in order to be crowned with the prize of victory to describe in Ph 3:13-14 how Christians can never stop growing but must desire and do all possible to attain greater union with Jesus Christ and lovingly serve others, as Christ did.

Epignosis: This is a favorite word of Paul to describe knowledge beyond any human understanding by the mind alone. It expresses the Hebrew word, *yada*, to describe "heart" knowledge that empowers the "poor in spirit" to respond to God's call by loving action. Such knowledge brings with it a commitment between loving friends.

Eschatology: This refers to the theological study, through Christian revelation, of the end of the world. It embraces such topics as death and resurrection, the last judgment with God's just retribution, the punishment of evildoers and the beatific vision of the Triune God by the redeemed. It embraces the topics of heaven, hell, and purgatory.

Eschaton: The Greek word for the end or the end times in which God's eternal plan will be fulfilled and the Kingdom of Heaven will be established in its fullness and manifested by all creatures in Christ.

Gnosis: This means "knowledge" in Greek. To Gnostic sects it meant to obtain through a secret ceremony a privileged knowledge that brought enlightenment. Paul uses it in a Christian sense to refer to Christian wisdom, both natural intellectual wisdom but also a supernatural wisdom given by the Holy Spirit that surpasses all human undertanding.

Gnosticism: This refers in Paul's time to those philosophical-mystical systems that existed before Christianity and represents the fusion of Oriental and Hellenic ideas into various elaborate systems whose aim is to acquire *gnosis* or knowledge of the divine. In the second century of Christianity it took on a heretical form with the Christian element only a superficial addition to a system already complete. It spread from Edessa and Alexandria and was refuted by many early Christian writers, especially St. Irenaeus of Lyons in his work, *Adversus Haereses.*

Kaine Ktisis: This means in Greek "a new creation." The essence of the initiation sacrament of Baptism is to fashion us into a "new creation" in Christ (2 Cor 5:17).

Kairos: This refers in Pauline thought to the new time of salvation, the graced moment which is made available to us as a result of Christ's resurrection and the Holy Spirit's coming to live in us.

Kerygma: This refers to the preaching of the Gospel, rooted in Christ's revelations to his first apostles, including Paul who received revelations directly from Christ.

Koinonia: Greek word meaning "community" or shared fellowship. In Christian writings it refers to the Church as a community, the Church sharing in the Trinitarian divine life, especially in and through the Eucharist. It is the work of the Holy Spirit to bring about such a community of love.

Kyrios: The meaning is "Lord, Master, God." Paul specifically uses it to refer to the risen Lord Jesus Christ whom the Father has glorified after Christ's death and exalted him as King of the Universe (cf. 1 Cor 12:4).

Logos: This means in Greek "word" or the form which expresses a thought as well as the thought itself. The early Greek Fathers built their Christology upon the writings of St. Paul and St. John, who stressed that Jesus Christ was the *Logos*, the fullest expression of God to the world. One with the Godhead from all eternity, the *Logos* took on himself our human nature. It is in the *Logos* in whom all things are created (Jn 1:2). Therefore every creature possesses a unique *logos* in relationship to the Divine *Logos*, Jesus Christ, who in the end will gather all creatures into himself and bring the universe to its fulfillment in God.

Metanoia: A conversion of one's whole being in total surrender to make the indwelling Trinity the total center of one's life through the permanent union of life in and with Christ through the guidance of the Holy Spirit.

Mysterion: This refers in the pagan mystery cults of Paul's time to the mystery which was a secret ceremony or a secret truth given to those initiated into these cults. Knowledge of these mysteries brought about a kind of salvific enlightenment. Paul uses this term to refer to the hidden work of God's decrees to save humankind through Jesus Christ and the Holy Spirit.

Mysticism: Evelyn Underhill gives us an apt definition of mysticism that well applies to the mystical view of St. Paul, even though he would not have understood the term as most modern persons use it: "Mysticism is the expression of the innate yearning of the human spirit towards total harmony with the transcendental order, whatever may be the theological formula in which this order is expressed" (*The School of Charity and the Mystery of Sacrifice*, p. 235).

Nekrosis: In Greek this means "death." Paul refers to this term as a putting to death all sin and living for God in Christ Jesus (Rm 6:11). This is a necessary discipline whereby we cooperate with the indwelling, risen Lord to remove and avoid all obstacles that may prevent our growth in holiness and greater union with Christ. The positive aspect is to develop by external and internal discipline the virtues which Christ developed in his earthly life.

Oikodome: This means "to build a house." Paul uses this metaphor in 2 Cor 5:1 to describe the "house" or person God has built us to be forever.

Omega: This is the last letter of the Greek alphabet. Paul uses it to refer to Christ as the goal and finality of all creation who will be manifested in the final *parousia* of Christ's Second Coming.

Pantokrator: This refers in Paul's writings to the risen Christ who is the "All-Powerful Ruler" over the univere. The Father has given to Christ risen all power over all created powers and principalities.

Parousia: In Greek this means "presence" or "manifestation" through a fulfillment, or the "arrival" of some high-ranking person. It denoted the triumphal entry of rulers, kings, emperors, high-ranking magistrates and religious leaders into a city. Paul uses it to refer to the triumphal entry of Christ in his victorous return to earth at the end of time (1 Th 5:2; 2 Th 1:7-12; 2:1-12; 1 Cor 15:20-28; 2 Cor 1:14).

Photizein: In Greek this means "to light up, to enlighten, to make radiant."

Physis: Greek for "nature" or "essence" of a being.

Pistis: Greek for "faith." Paul uses this word to refer to faith as more than a mere intellectual assent to a truth revealed by God. Paul sees the Christian's authentic *faith* to be like that of Abraham, a loving response to God's revelation and call given to an individual and to the community. It is the foundation for the virtues of *hope* and *love*.

Pleroma: This means "fullness" or "maturity." In Paul's writings it refers both to the fulfillment in unity of God's entire cosmic creation as well as the primary *telos* or goal which God, through his two hands, "Jesus Christ and his Holy Spirit" in Irenaeus' words, seeks to bring about in the end times or in the *eschaton*.

Pneuma: This is the term found in the Old and New Testaments to refer to "spirit" or "breath." Paul uses it in his often repeated antithesis between flesh and spirit. We become "spiritual" or "pneumatic" when we are guided by the Holy Spirit.

Praxis: The Greek word for "deed, act, or action." In Paul's ascetical teaching *praxis* refers to what human beings do in cooperation with God's grace in order to uproot any self-centeredness manifested in general by the eight "vices" and to put on the mind of Jesus Christ by an inner revolution (Eph 4:17) by positively developing the virtues he lived by and taught us to imitate in the Gospel.

Sarx: "Flesh." Paul uses this term to represent human beings, not only in their creatureliness as mortal and weak, but also in their estrangement from God through sin.

Soma: "Body." For Paul it means more than the material body of a person. It points to the whole, human individual in his or her potential for action in the temporal world. Thus our resurrected body will be a spiritualized, "embodied" being in union with the gloriously risen Christ, in obedience to God to serve him in truth and love in the life to come.

Soteria & Soter: *Soteria* means "salvation" or "redemption." Fundamentally it means to bring one to safety. In Christianity it refers to the branch of theology, *Soteriology*, that seeks to explain how Jesus Christ has brought about the salvation of the human race. He is referred to by the Greek word, *Soter*, the Savior.

Sphragis: This means "to be sealed, signed or stamped" by the Holy Spirit so that we can belong totally to Christ (e.g. Eph 1:13).

Synergy: This comes from the Greek prefix, *syn*, meaning "with" and the word, *energeia*, meaning, "a working." It refers to Paul's teaching about Jesus' working with the Father, as well as our own human cooperation with him who is the head of the body, the Church, to build up the Kingdom of God.

Zoopoion: This word comes from the Greek, *zoe* and *poion*, meaning the "lifegiver." It refers, in Paul's writings, to the Holy Spirit.

A SELECTED BIBLIOGRAPHY

Amiot, François. *The Key Concepts of St. Paul* (NY: Herder & Herder, 1962).

Augrain, Charles. *Paul, Master of the Spiritual Life*, Vols. 1 & 2, tr. Sr. M. Paul Purcell (Staten Island, NY: Alba House, 1968).

Banks, R. *Paul's Idea of Community* (Exeter: Paternoster, 1980).

Barrett, C.K. *From First Adam to Last, A Study in Pauline Theology* (NY: Scribner, 1962).

Cerfaux, Lucien. *Christ in the Theology of St. Paul*, tr. Geoffrey Webb & Adrian Walker (NY: Herder & Herder, 1962).

_____. *The Christian in the Theology of St. Paul* (NY: Herder & Herder, 1967).

Deissmann, Adolf. *Paul: A Study in Social and Religious History*, tr. William E. Wilson (NY: Harper & Bros. Publishers, 1957).

Gundry, R.H. *'Soma' in Biblical Theology with Emphasis on Pauline Anthropology* (Cambridge: Cambridge University Press, 1976).

Huby, Joseph, SJ. *Mystique Pauliniénne et Johannique* (Paris: Desclée de Brouwer, 1946).

Jewett, R. *A Chronology of Paul's Life* (Philadelphia: Fortress Press, 1979).

Montague, George T., SM. *Maturing in Christ: St. Paul's Program for Christian Growth* (Milwaukee: Bruce Publishing Company, 1964).

Prat, F. *The Theology of St. Paul*, tr. J.L. Stoddard, 5th ed. Vol. II
     (London, 1945).

Schweitzer, A. *Mysticism of Paul the Apostle* (London, 1953).

Scott, Charles, A.A. *Christianity According to St. Paul* (Cambridge:
     Cambridge Univ. Press, 1961).

Scroggs, R. *The Last Adam* (Oxford, Blackwell, 1966).

Taylor, L.H. *The New Creation* (NY: Pageant Press, 1958).

Taylor, Michael J., SJ. *Paul: His Letters, Message and Heritage* (NY:
     Alba House, 1997).

Wikenhauser, Alfred. *Pauline Mysticism. Christ in the Mystical
     Teaching of St. Paul*, tr. Joseph Cunningham (NY:
     Herder & Herder, 1956).